THE GOSPEL OF
BRIAN MCLAREN

THE GOSPEL OF BRIAN MCLAREN

A New Kind of Christianity for a Multi-Faith World

JEREMY BOUMA

"Who do you say that I am?"
-Jesus Christ

RENEW WEST MICHIGAN
Every purchase will help support
new West Michigan church plants.
Learn more at www.theoklesia.com/renew

The Gospel of Brian McLaren: A New Kind of Christianity for a Multi-Faith World

© 2013 by Jeremy Bouma

Part 1 content adapted from *Reimagining the Kingdom: The Generational Development of Liberal* Kingdom *Grammar from Schleiermacher to McLaren*. Copyright © 2012 by Jeremy Bouma

Published by **THEOKLESIA**
P.O. Box 1180
Grand Rapids, MI 49501
www.theoklesia.com

Scripture quotations taken from The Holy Bible, New International Version®. NIV®. Copyright © 1973, 1978, 1984, 2011 by Biblica, Inc.TM Used by permission. All rights reserved worldwide.

Cover Bible image from Billy Alexander/stock.xchng. Used by permission.

ISBN: 978-0-6157328-9-3

Printed in the United States of America

10 09 08 07 06 05 04 03 02 01

About **THEOKLESIA**

We are a content curator dedicated to helping the 21st century Church rediscover the historic Christian faith. Jesus said that the Church is "the light of the world, a city on a hill that cannot be hidden." We provide the resources to help Her shine brightly in the 21st century by helping the Church connect God's Story of Rescue to our cities, while remaining theologically rooted and biblically uncompromising.

www.theoklesia.com • info@theoklesia.com

CONTENTS

PART 2: A New Kind of Christianity for a Multi-Faith World

PREFACE

The first time I met Brian McLaren was the day I visited his church, Cedar Ridge Community Church. I was living in the Washington D.C. area and just left an area megachurch I had been part of for a few years. I left because I had entered a period of faith deconstruction and reconstruction the likes of which I had never experienced before—and this was largely thanks to Pastor Brian, or should I say Pastor Dan and his faith-deconstruction mentor Neil Oliver. While I lived nearly 40 minutes away, I felt drawn to this mini-mecca of Emergent and its good-natured prophet to experience first hand his teaching and insight into a new way of being a Christian, a new kind of Christianity.

I remember Brian greeting me as I sat pensively in an aisle seat a few rows back from the front. There he was, shaking my hand, with his infectious grin, small Buddha belly, and trademark close-cropped beard that flowed up around his balding head. He was sort of like Santa, but without that sack of toys, or long shimmery silver beard. We exchanged a few words—he asked me what I did in the city and I mentioned the organization I worked for was a ministry to politicians, which piqued his interest. Unfortunately, our conversation was cut short by the start of the service. Afterwards, I stayed for the new visitors meeting, where I got a sweet CRCC mug, which I still have somewhere in some basement box. That was my first encounter with Brian, but not my last.

A few months later, Brian helped launch a movement in the DC area, called *Worship in the Spirit of Justice*. The worship gathering event was a 5-week long series of non-violent protest worship-ins to bear prophetic witness to the atrocities committed in Sudan, particularly Darfur. Think Occupy Wall Street without all the tents and latrines. We met at strategic points around Washington—the Lincoln memorial, Capitol Building, Washington Press Club, the Sudan embassy, and White House—to worship, read Scripture (or from "sacred texts," more on that below), and pray for the genocide a continent away.

Along with his good friend Jim Wallis, several people from Sojourners, and other religious leaders in the area, Brian launched this movement after being deeply impacted by the movie *Hotel Rwanda*. As he sat in utter silence and disbelief as that movie chronicled Rwandan genocide, he vowed he would never again sit idly by while something similar was happening during his lifetime.

While at the time I appreciated Brian's gumption and valued the opportunity to lend my worship and prayers to this prophetic movement, looking back there were aspects that were, shall we say...odd. One came during the final week, which was held in a park just north of the White House. This final prophetic protest was particularly memorable because of the actors who shared the stage: along with Christian pastors and a Jewish rabbi was a Muslim imam who prayed, to Allah, and read from the Koran. It was as if we—Christian, Jew, and Muslim—were all worshiping and praying to the same God. This was the first time I realized things were a bit off, but it wouldn't be the last.

Years later, when I moved back to Grand Rapids to pursue seminary, I attended a national pastors conference in San Diego. Before the actual event started, there were several pre-conference workshops, one of which Brian led based on his newest book, *Everything Must Change*. Huddled around Brian were a handful of pastors who, like me, were interested in his sage wisdom and advice for ministering in an emerging postmodern world. And he was eager to dispense to us that wisdom. Using his handy dry-eraser board, Brian spent several hours illustrating the greatest tragedies threatening human existence, and how to solve them.

What struck me as odd during this third encounter was how Brian defined our human problem and solution: Our problem was not our personal rebellion against God (a.k.a. sin), but broad systems of injustice that oppress people from the outside and model for them a bad existence; our solution was not faith in Jesus Christ as Lord and Savior (carrying with that belief in who He is as the only one true God and what He did in life, death, and resurrection), but faith in the *way* of Jesus and His model for a better existence. In other words, I was struck by the shift in his understanding of the gospel and fundamentals of the Christian faith. I wouldn't fully understand this shift until two years later when I began to immerse myself in historical theology and when Brian fully revealed his theological hand with his magnum opus: *A New Kind of Christianity.*

This book launched February 9, 2010 with fervent cries on either side of the theological aisle. Some backslapped Brian for his theological courage. Others just slapped him for challenging historic Christian orthodoxy. Personally, I was shocked at where Brian had ended up theologically, and decided to spend several weeks reviewing the book on my blog, www.novuslumen.net. Here is what I wrote in a shorter review:

> I've struggled with how to introduce this review because of how much I've struggled with the book. Yes, I've struggled with the ideas and theology and writing itself. For me it's more than that:
>
> I don't get it.
>
> I don't understand what happened. How did Brian get from THERE <-----to-----> HERE? The Brian of ANKofXianity doesn't seem like the same guy who launched this whole Emergent journey nearly a decade ago. The man behind this book just doesn't seem like the guy I encountered in his first-ever book, The Church on

the Other Side, the man who was as generous in his orthodoxy as he was genuinely appreciative toward orthodoxy itself, and the wandering, yet tethered, theo-explorer I found in his mythic characters Neo or Pastor Dan.

Now don't get me wrong. I don't know Brian McLaren. I've had a few encounters and conversations with him, like at some sessions at the National Pastors Conference a year ago. But I also attended his church for half a year and was involved in a social justice project he helped coordinate while in Washington D.C. Here's the thing: I leapt into his church and into this social activism because I trusted Brian and his voice. While wading through my own spiritual deconstruction process five years ago, I gravitated to the only person I knew who was asking the questions I was asking, but seemed tethered to the "pieces" that still mattered to the Christian faith. I respected him for his prophetic voice and when people bleated and bellowed on and on about his so-called "heresy," I defended. I went to the mat with my boss in ministry, skeptical friends, and mortified parents.

So when I ask, "what happened?" I ask the question as one who was, to some extent, personally invested. Sure I man-crushed on the guy a bit to hard, but I sought his wisdom and insight and church community to help me navigate the terra nova at the intersection of postmodernity and Christian spirituality. I saw in Brian a desire to peal away the crap the USAmerican Church attached to Jesus and the Cross, while not cashing in the farm completely.

That, however, has changed.

While I know I have shifted in my own spiritual/ theological journey, it is clear Brian has progressively shifted, too. I highly doubt Brian would have guessed 28 years ago at the beginning of his pastoral Christian ministry that he would push a new kind of Christianity that scantily reflects the Holy Scriptures and subverts the historical Rule of Faith that believes Jesus Christ is exclusively Lord and Messiah. Unfortunately, this seems to be the case.

Though Brian wonders aloud "How did a mild-manner guy like me get into so much trouble" (2) and insists he "never planned to become a `controversial religious leader,'" (3) he is the one to blame. He is the one who has shifted and engaged in this current theological endeavor. This theological enterprise is not accidentally garnering unwarranted criticism because there is nothing accidental about Brian's theological endeavor: Brian's book is a bold, intentional rhetorical tour de force that strikes at the very heart of the historic Christian faith, parodying the faith that both the Communion of Saints and the Spirit of God has given the 21st Century Church; his work pushes a version of Christianity that falls far outside the witness of the Holy Scriptures to Jesus Christ as exclusive Lord and Savior.

His portrayal of conservative evangelicalism is a gross caricature and unworthy of any serious thinker. He deliberately exaggerates and distorts the theology and exegesis of those with whom he disagrees in order to create an easy rhetorical jab called a Straw Man. As you probably know, a Straw Man is a logical fallacy that intentionally misrepresents an opponents position in order to easily strike it down in order to give the illusion that said opponent is defeated. Such rhetorical devices litter this book, making it an unworthy conversational partner.

Brian makes grand, sweeping claims with skimpy-to-no scholarly support. Perhaps this is why he insists over and over and over again that he had no formal seminary training? This is one of the most frustrating aspects of a book that asks us to take it seriously. For instance, his Greco-Roman narrative claims came to him not through research and scholarly reading, but through two conversations with two separate friends. (37)

Brian's interaction with the Holy Scriptures has no exegetical methodology. Instead he simply asks the reader to take his word for it. For example, his exegesis of John 14:6 is so innovative that he could find no commentary support for it. His presupposition re: the audience of The Book of Romans is just flat out wrong; the consensus among commentators is that Paul wrote the letter to converted Gentile Christians, not Jews.

While Brian claims otherwise, the new version of Christianity he pushes bears little to no resemblance to historic Christian orthodoxy, especially Nicene Christianity. In fact, he claims the creeds were mandated by the emperor to promote unity in the church and bring about imperial control. (12) Furthermore, by shoving Christian orthodoxy into his "Christian religion" rhetorical device, he is able to transcend the Christian faith entirely with a generalized "Kingdom of God" motif.

His portrayal of the Biblical narrative is Christless, centering squarely on Abraham and the Kingdom of God (which fits nicely with his view of the Abrahamic faiths as encapsulated in the nonprofit Abrahamic Alliance, on which he sits as Board member).

His view of Jesus Christ in no way affirms that He is God. Instead Brian reduces Him to a revelation of the "character of God." Jesus is no more than a model citizen.

His view of the Holy Scripture is not divine revelation, but purely human conversations in which people simple talk about their understanding of God and progressively, courageously "trade-up' (his words not mine) their understanding of God for even better images. Brian follows Pete Rollins' suggestion that our understanding of God is not actually the knowledge of God, but simply our understanding of God. Does God present Himself to us in the Text? Is He even saying anything to us in it? Can we really possess the knowledge of God? These questions seem to have a negative answer, though it isn't clear.

He rarely uses Jesus' messianic designation (Christ), which reflects his refusal to acknowledge Jesus Christ as exclusive Lord and Messiah. (So far he uses "Jesus" 204 times, "Jesus Christ" 3 time, and "Christ" 11 times.)

He consistently preemptively belittles those who will push against his innovative, new Christianity through gross ad hominems by reducing us to "gatekeepers" (103) anxious and paranoid (212-213), "religious thought police" (85), brainwashers (48), and people who are vulnerable to repeating yesterday's atrocities in the future (including anti-Semitism, genocide, and witch burning) (85), among many others charges.

While Brian feigns theological innocence by merely offering a "new way of believing," rather than a new set of beliefs (18), make no mistake about it: Brian is absolutely, unambiguously offering new beliefs. Though he may insist he is merely offering questions to inspire new conversations in the interest of a new quest, (18) he knows exactly what he is doing. He is disingenuous when he insists he is merely offering responses to his questions, rather than answers.

In the end, Brian's McLarenism faith isn't really about Jesus Christ, but about a vanilla, generalized World-Spirit god that has visited all other religions outside the Christian faith. Like his good buddy, Samir Selmanovic, Brian believes that Jesus and the reconciliation God offers to the world is not found only in the Christian faith (or "religion" as he puts it). In Selmonvic's book (a book Brian endorsed), Samir says, "We do believe that God is best defined by the historical revelation in Jesus Christ, but to believe that God is limited to it would be an attempt to manage God. If one holds that Christ is confined to Christianity, one has chosen a god that is not sovereign." (It's Really All About God, 129) Brian agrees.

In fact, it is clear his entire theological endeavor is a concerted effort to "pluralize" reconciliation to God and His Kingdom by divorcing it from Jesus Christ entirely, rather than insisting that reconciliation to both comes through Jesus Christ alone. While Brian uses the "Christian religion" as a rhetorical device to argue against "theo-containment," the One True God described in the Holy Scriptures is exclusively revealed in the very human, very divine Jesus Christ. It's really not all about God. It's really all about Jesus Christ.

As Karl Barth reminds us, "Any deviation, any attempt to evade Jesus Christ in favor of another supposed revelation of God, or any denial of the fulness of God's presence in Him, will precipitate us into darkness and confusion."(CD II,1:319) There is little evidence Brian believes that the fulness of God's presence is exclusively in Jesus Christ, that salvation and rescue and reconciliation is found in no other name under heaven besides His.

After Jesus, there is nothing left. And after Brian's new kind of Christianity, neither is Jesus Christ.

While I had a strong sense at the time that Brian had completely jumped ship from historic Christian orthodoxy, my sense wasn't entirely confirmed until my Master of Theology program in historical theology culminated with my thesis. I chose my topic based on a growing sense of mission to interact with Emergent theology in order to better understand the roots from which it has grown. One of the biggest theological concepts of the Emergent Church has been a hyper-focus on the Kingdom of God. Furthermore, it isn't a secret that people have labeled Emergent theology liberalism in evangelical clothing. So I set out to prove whether Emergent understandings of the Kingdom were similar to or different from theological liberal views of the Kingdom. What I discovered was staggering.

Using Brian as a theological representative of Emergent theology—an entirely appropriate representative at that—I discovered that his theological views concerning a range of ideas continue the theological impulse and trajectory of liberalism, four generations deep. (This thesis project was released in 2012 as a print book and ebook under the title, *Reimagining the Kingdom: The Generational Development of*

Liberal Kingdom Grammar.) Along with Friedrich Schleiermacher, Albrecht Ritschl, Walter Rauschenbusch, and Paul Tillich, Brian McLaren's view of our human problem (sin), the solution to our problem (salvation and the Kingdom) and the bearer of our solution (the person and work of Jesus) is nearly identical. The only difference is that Brian's theological system revises and extends liberal Kingdom grammar for a postmodern, multi-faith world. No clearer do we see this than in his latest book, *Why Did Jesus, Moses, the Buddha, and Mohammed Cross the Road?: Christian Identity in a Multi-Faith World.*

This revision and extension is why I've released this short book. It contains the chapter on Brian's theological system from my Kingdom book and a summary and evaluation of his arguments from this new book on religious pluralism. While I trace the development of Brian's liberal theology through four generations of theological liberals beforehand, this chapter on its own in Part 1 should give you a good handle on what Brian believes, and how it is foreign to the historic Christian faith. (If you'd like the full argument, you may purchase the book from most online retailers.) Part 2 contains the summary and evaluation of Brian's arguments in his latest book in order to show how his gospel is indeed a new kind of Christianity for a multi-faith world.

In the Book of Jude, the author urges the church to "contend for the faith that was once for all entrusted to God's holy people." (Jude 3) I believe now, more than ever, we need people who are passionate about safeguarding that once-for-all entrusted faith. Part of the way we can contend for that faith is to better understand the theological roots of people like Brian McLaren. Though his influence has waned as the Emergent Church movement has fizzled, he is still a prominent voice in many corners of the American church. Such prominence and influence requires a thoughtful interaction with his gospel. And because that gospel is foreign to the historic Christian faith, a forceful response is also required. I hope this short book will provide both.

JEREMY BOUMA
GRAND RAPIDS • FEBRUARY 2013

PART 1

McLaren's *Kingdom* Grammar

THE GOSPEL OF BRIAN MCLAREN

INTRODUCTION

In recent years evangelical Christians have rediscovered the biblical emphasis on the Kingdom of God. They have written books, such as *The King Jesus Gospel*,[1] *The Secret Message of Jesus*,[2] and *The Next Christians*,[3] which remind evangelicals that the Kingdom of God lies at the heart of Jesus'

---

[1] Scot McKnight, *The King Jesus Gospel: The Original Good News Revisited* (Grand Rapids: Zondervan, 2011).

[2] Brian McLaren, *The Secret Message of Jesus* (Nashville: W Publishing Group, 2006).

[3] Gabe Lyons, *The Next Christians: The Good News About the End of Christian America* (New York: Doubleday, 2010).

mission. They lead mission trips which seek to do more than merely lead sinners to Jesus; they also want to bring the Kingdom of God to earth. In many ways this rediscovery of the Kingdom is right and beneficial, for its advent is the overarching plot line of the Bible. However, its current use often comes with problematic baggage as many of its most popular proponents uncritically borrow its grammar from unorthodox historical sources.

The Kingdom of God has not always played such a prominent role in Christian theology, however. Augustine represents the typical manner in which the early church defined the Kingdom of God, equating it with the Church itself. While equating God's Kingdom-rule with the Church largely continued with medieval theological discourse, Christian princes sought to promote an imperial-political view of the Kingdom in order to control their Feudal lands. In the Reformation, Luther individualized the concept for the purpose of emphasizing the Christian's spiritual citizenship over against a citizenship of a secular kingdom. He also represented the Reformation tendency in general to view the Kingdom in entirely eschatological, even apocalyptic, terms that pointed toward heaven in the future. Eventually, the Kingdom played little role in Protestant theology, especially evangelical theology, reflecting the general trajectory of the historic Church that seems to have had little interest in Jesus' central teaching. That is until the nineteenth century.

In the late eighteenth century and early nineteenth century, historical, cultural, and intellectual forces coalesced to foster an environment that gave renewed interest in the

Kingdom, giving it a place of theological prominence. The person most credited with such renewal is the German theologian Friedrich Schleiermacher. The Kingdom of God formed the basis of his teachings, governing his system of doctrine and ethics to such an extent that it rose to prominence within theology in a way it had not before. Schleiermacher's voice echoed throughout much of nineteenth century Protestant thought through the likes of Bauer, Herrmann, and Harnack, finding a strong advocate in the theology of Albrecht Ritschl. But while Ritschl praised Schleiermacher for employing the Kingdom of God as the *telos* of Christianity, he believed Schleiermacher did not go far enough in grasping its significance. Ritschl believed Schleiermacher made an important contribution to Christian theology by restoring the Kingdom to a place of importance, but he thought his *Kingdom* grammar was deficient. Building on the original work of Schleiermacher, Ritschl brought this grammar to bear on his entire theological enterprise, making *Kingdom of God* its controlling doctrine. Ritschl's Kingdom-centric theology kindled a new generation of twentieth century liberal theologians, particularly Rauschenbusch and Tillich, who envisioned the Kingdom itself as humanity's salvation.

Now, like the nineteenth century, there has been a resurgence in the use of *Kingdom* language at the start of the twenty-first century, particularly within mainstream evangelicalism. In prior generations, *Kingdom* had not been part of the normal evangelical ecclesial repertoire. Instead, evangelicalism had primarily centered upon the language of *gospel*, which translated into salvation from sins through a conversion experience, personal piety, and moral living. Rarely had *Kingdom* language been employed within evangelicalism. Even when *Kingdom* was utilized, its primary usage was usually future oriented, centering on the return of Jesus Christ and reign on earth at the expense of its present activity. This definition of *Kingdom*, however, changed with the advent of what has become known as the Emergent Church movement, originally a progressive evangelical movement that sought to re-imagine traditional Christianity in light of postmodernity. In fact, the Kingdom of God is central to the Emergent Church's protest against Traditionalism.

As Jim Belcher explains, "The emerging protest argues that the traditional church has focused too much attention on *how* an individual becomes saved and not enough on how he or she *lives* as a Christian...The critics say the good news is more than forgiveness from sins and a ticket to heaven; it is the appearance of the kingdom of God."[4] This argument, that not enough attention has been paid to Jesus' teaching on the Kingdom of God, has formed the beachhead of protest against Traditionalism, particularly mainstream evangelicalism, and is the central identifying doctrine of this movement. As two prominent Emergent researchers note, the Kingdom of God offers a "reference point for emerging churches" as they deconstruct Traditionalism and reconstruct church in a

---

[4] Jim Belcher, *Deep Church: A Third Way Beyond Emerging and Traditional* (Downers Grove: IVP Books, 2009), 41.

postmodern context.[5]   The Kingdom-way Jesus founded through His life provides a model for emerging churches and actually is their gospel; for them, the Kingdom saves. No thinker within this movement has sought to redirect the focus of twenty-first century Christianity more than Brian McLaren, who helped found the national organization Emergent, is the author of several books that have set out to re-imagine the Christian faith,[6] and was christened as one of the top twenty-five most influential evangelicals in America.[7] For some time, McLaren has been on a quest to redefine what is central to the Christian faith, a quest culminating with a new book on Christian identity in a multi-faith world.[8]

---

[5]   Eddie Gibbs and Ryan K. Bolger. *Emerging Churches: Creating Christian Community in Postmodern Culture* (Grand Rapids: BakerAcademic, 2005), 46. This book provided one of the most exhaustive examinations of the Emerging Church movement. It especially provides an important look at the Emerging Church's *Kingdom* grammar in p. 47-64.

[6] See *A New Kind of Christian* (San Francisco: Jossey-Bass, 2001); *The Story We Find Ourselves In* (San Francisco: Jossey-Bass, 2003); *The Last Word and The Word After That* (San Francisco: Jossey-Bass, 2005); *A Generous Orthodoxy* (Grand Rapids: Zondervan, 2004); *The Secret Message of Jesus* (Nashville: W Publishing Group, 2006); *Everything Must Change* (Nashville: Thomas Nelson, 2006); and *A New Kind of Christianity* (New York: HarperOne, 2010).

[7]   "25 Most Influential Evangelicals In America," *Time Magazine*, February 7, 2005.

[8] Brian McLaren, *Why Did Jesus, Moses, the Buddah, and Mohammed Cross the Road? Christian Identity in a Multi-Faith World*   (Jericho Books, New York, 2012)

Over the past decade, McLaren has sought to reclaim what he calls the secret, essential message of Jesus, which he says has been unintentionally misunderstood and intentionally distorted, missed and disregarded.[9] According to McLaren, this message is the Kingdom of God. While many have lauded McLaren's efforts to recapture Jesus' secret Kingdom-message, others argue that his and Emergent's use and description of *Kingdom* is deficient. Belcher writes, "I worry about what is missing in the description [of the Kingdom of God]. It is curious to me that nowhere does he mention or link the kingdom of God to the doctrines of atonement, justification, union with Christ or our need to be forgiven."[10] Likewise, Scot McKnight believes what McLaren says about the Kingdom is not enough:

> [They] believe that penal substitution theories have not led to a kingdom vision. What I have been pondering and writing about for a decade now is how to construct an 'emerging' gospel that remains faithful to the fulness of the biblical texts about the Atonement, and lands squarely on the word *kingdom*. Girard said something important about the Cross; so does McLaren. But they aren't enough.[11]

---

9 McLaren, *The Secret Message of Jesus*, 3.

10 Belcher, *Deep Church*, 118.

11 Scot McKnight, "McLaren Emerging," *Christianity Today Online*, September 26, 2008, www.christianitytoday.com/ct/2008/september/38.59.html.

The reason contemporary articulations of *Kingdom* by Emergents like McLaren are not enough is because those articulations are simply appropriations of liberal *Kingdom* grammar.

Rather than offering the Church a new kind of Christianity that somehow recaptures a long-lost concept central to Jesus and the Church, McLaren's use of the Kingdom of God to define the Christian gospel is fully entrenched in the Protestant liberal theological tradition, a link several people have already noted. In his book, *Don't Stop Believing,* Michael Wittmer argues that a "postmodern turn toward liberalism is penetrating the evangelical church." He goes on to say that "an increasing number of postmodern Christians are practicing a liberal method: accommodating the gospel to contemporary culture and expressing greater concern for Christian ethics than its traditional doctrines,"[12] including the Kingdom of God.[13]

In reviewing one of his latest books, *A New Kind of Christianity,* McKnight notes how McLaren "has fallen for an old school of thought," rehashing the ideas of prominent classic Protestant liberals like Adolf Von Harnack and modern ones like Harvey Cox.[14] McKnight has registered such a

---

[12] Michael E. Wittmer, *Don't Stop Believing: Why Living Like Jesus is Not Enough* (Grand Rapids: Zondervan, 2008), 18.

[13] See Wittmer, *Don't Stop Believing,* 110-115.

[14] Scot McKnight, "Review: Brian McLaren's 'A New Kind of Christianity,'" *Christianity Today Online*, February 26, 2010, http://www.christianitytoday.com/ct/2010/march/3.59.html.

concern in regards to McLaren's *Kingdom* definition, as well.[15] Likewise, Belcher worries about what is missing in McLaren's description of the Kingdom, noting that his definition reduces the gospel and argues that if his gospel is nothing more than recycled theological liberalism it must be rejected.[16]

This small book, adapted from my larger book, *Reimagining the Kingdom*,[17] shows how McLaren's gospel of the Kingdom is continuous with four previous generations of Protestant liberalism, including how he defines the Kingdom of God, who is in, how one gets in, and how it solves for our human problem. The larger book traces the generational development of liberal *Kingdom* grammar from Friedrich Schleiermacher to Albrecht Ritschl, Walter Rauschenbusch, and Paul Tillich, to show how the *Kingdom* grammar of Emergent is more or less repackaged liberal grammar. By examining the most prominent Protestant liberals, I demonstrate a direct link between them and Emergent and show how they are contributing to the comeback of evangelical *Kingdom* grammar, as evidenced in McLaren's *Kingdom* grammar.

Theological liberals are remarkably similar in their definitions of our human problem, the One who bore that

---

[15] McKnight, "McLaren Emerging," www.christianitytoday.com/ct/2008/september/38.59.html.

[16] Belcher, *Deep Church*, 116.

[17] Jeremy Bouma, *Reimagining the Kingdom: The Generational Development of Liberal* Kingdom *Grammar from Schleiermacher to McLaren* (Grand Rapids: THEOKLESIA, 2012)

problem's solution, and the nature of that solution itself, the Kingdom of God. This small book features the chapter on McLaren from this larger book on the development of Kingdom grammar. In it, you will see that, while the McLaren claims to be helping Christianity rediscover an authentic Christian identity by rediscovering the Kingdom, he is merely repackaging liberalism for a new day; his gospel is the liberal gospel.

McLaren's grammar includes several features from theological liberalism: He teaches that sin is social and environmental, rather than an inherited sinful nature and guilt; Jesus is the moral, rather than metaphysical, Son of God; in founding the Kingdom of God, it was necessary that Jesus lived but he gives no compelling reason that Jesus' death was necessary; the Kingdom of God is concerned with humanity's progress; the Kingdom comes into the here-and-now through the power of loving human action; it is inclusive, in that every act counts as Kingdom acts; it is universalistic, in that everyone will be saved; the Kingdom centers on the words, deeds, and suffering of Jesus—His inspiring personality provides humanity the proper example of the universal human ideal; and ultimately, the Kingdom is concerned with bringing the universal human ideal to bear on human existence, empowering individuals and society to reach their fullest potential and live their best life right now.

McLaren's *Kingdom* grammar, and thus *gospel* grammar, is continuous with four previous generations of Protestant liberalism, including how he defines the Kingdom of God, who is in, how one gets in, and how it solves for our human problem. Like the liberal gospel, McLaren's gospel ultimately urges people to place their faith in the *way* of Jesus—i.e. the Kingdom of God—rather than the *person* and *work* of Jesus. This is a significant departure from authentic, historic Christianity.

Roger Olson has said that the story of Christian theology is the story of Christian reflection on the nature of salvation, which is why this book is important. It is imperative that evangelicals understand the contours of McLaren's gospel in order to understand how he could impact how some evangelicals reflect upon the nature of salvation, and consequently how they understand, show, and tell the gospel itself in our multi-faith world.

2

CONTEXT

How Did McLaren's Gospel Form?

In 2001 Brian McLaren, a little known pastor just north of Washington D.C., began influencing street-level theological conversations within evangelicalism with his landmark book, *A New Kind of Christian.* [1] Through the book's two protagonists—Pastor Dan and Neo—McLaren took the reader on a redefining journey through evangelical's core theological doctrines. God, creation, sin, Christ, the cross, resurrection,

---

[1] McLaren has since retired from pastoring *Cedar Ridge Community Church* and been named one of the "25 Most Influential Evangelicals In America," *Time Magazine*, February 7, 2005.

and judgment were all addressed and countered with alternative possibilities that formed the foundation for the Emerging Church conversation. It was also a reflection of his own spiritual journey, one that began with fundamentalism via the Plymouth Brethren and culminated in "a quest for honesty, for authenticity, and for a faith that made more sense to me and to others...learning that there is a kind of faith that runs deeper than mere beliefs."[2] Many in our post-9/11, recession-racked, socially-upended world who entered this church conversation found resonance with McLaren's own spiritual quest.

Those seeking to do Christianity on the other side of modernity have found solace in the questions and alternative answers offered by McLaren in response to what many perceive to be stogy, stuffy, stale theology that has outlived its lifecycle. In place of a theology he claims is beholden to modernity, McLaren insists "we need a new way of believing, not simply new answers to the same old questions, but a new set of questions. We are acknowledging that the Christianities we have created deserve to be reexamined and deconstructed...so that our religious traditions can be seen for what they are...they are evolving, embodied, situated versions of the faith."[3] Like other Emergents, McLaren has set out to construct a new, fresh, alternative Christianity in light of

---

[2] McLaren, *A New Kind of Christianity*, 6, 8.

[3] McLaren, *A New Kind of Christianity*, 18, 27.

postmodernity, because he like others realized "something isn't working in the way we're doing Christianity any more."[4]

Of postmodernism, McLaren writes, "I see the postmodern conversation as a profoundly moral project in intension at least, a kind of corporate repentance among European intellectuals in the decades after the Holocaust."[5] In embracing the *generous orthodoxy* descriptor of Hans Frei, McLaren embraces a post-foundationalism posture characteristic of postmodernism to describe his flavor of Christianity.[6] Postmodernism as an intellectual movement surfaced in the late 1960s as a surrogate to the post-structuralism of France, which itself was rooted in Kantian philosophy.[7] As Carl Raschke explains, "Postmodernism in this sense was nothing more or less than a theory of language that served to demystify previous theories of language routinely utilized to undercut the language of belief,"[8] particularly the "language of belief" rooted in modernity. Stanley Grenz notes, "postmodernism signifies the quest to move beyond modernism. Specifically, it involves a rejection

---

[4] McLaren, *A New Kind of Christianity*, 9.

[5] Brian McLaren, "Church Emerging: Or Why I Still Use the Word *Postmodern* but with Mixed Feelings," in *An Emergent Manifesto of Hope* (Ed. Doug Pagitt and Tony Jones; Grand Rapids: BakerBooks, 2007, 144.

[6] See McLaren, *A Generous Orthodoxy.*

[7] Carl Raschke, *The Next Reformation: Why Evangelicals Must Embrace Postmodernity* (Grand Rapids: Baker Academic, 2004), 35, 37.

[8] Raschke, *The Next Reformation*, 37.

of the modern-mindset, but launched under the conditions of modernity."[9] Grenz goes on to describe how the modern mind is defined by the Enlightenment project, which exalted the individual rational man to the center of the universe. The goal of the human intellectual quest was "to unlock the secrets of the universe in order to master nature for human benefit and create a better world," an ethos that particularly characterized the twentieth century through technology.[10] Postmodernism, on the other hand, says there can be no objective, autonomous knower because knowledge is not mechanistic and dualistic, but historical, relational, communal, and personal; reality is relative, indeterminate, intuited and participatory.[11] Three names are almost routinely associated with the postmodern project: Jacque Derrida, Jean François Lyotard, and Michael Foucault.

Derrida is considered the father of French deconstruction, a method for rethinking long held beliefs and intellectual assumptions. One of his primary contributions to postmodern philosophy was his often repeated phrase: "there is nothing outside the text." Here, Derrida champions the postmodern sentiment that interpretation is an inescapable part of being human and experiencing the world; life is interpretation all the way down because we all bring something to the table out of our cultural, economic, and

---

[9]Stanley Grenz, *A Primer on Postmodernism* (Grand Rapids: Eerdmans Publishing, 1996), 2.

[10] Stanley Grenz, *A Primer on Postmodernism*, 3.

[11] Stanley Grenz, *A Primer on Postmodernism*, 7-8.

religious context. For postmoderns, no realm of pure reading exists beyond the realm of interpretation.

Lyotard is known for his "incredulity toward metanarratives," which isn't so much a rejection of grand stories, but the manner in which those stories legitimize themselves. In other words, it is not the stories themselves that are the problem, but the way they are told (and to a degree why they are told). As James K. A. Smith argues, "For Lyotard, metanarratives are a distinctly modern phenomenon: they are stories that not only tell a grand story, but claim to be able to legitimate or prove the story's claim by an appeal to universal reason."[12] Smith continues, "What characterizes the postmodern condition, then, is not a rejection of grand stories in terms of scope or in the sense of epic claims, but rather an unveiling that all knowledge is rooted in some narrative or myth. The result, however, is what Lyotard describes as a 'problem of legitimation' since what we thought were universal criteria have been unveiled as just one game among many."[13] All claims to universal truth are reduced to one story among many stories. These stories are conditioned by their own sets of cultural and historical rules, a point McLaren and other Emergent Christians are quick to point out.

Finally, Foucault, the master institutional de-constructor was famous for his often quoted phrase, "power is knowledge." Foucault led the charge in cultivating a "deep hermeneutic of

---

[12] James K. A. Smith, *Who's Afraid of Postmodernism* (Grand Rapids: Baker Academic, 2006), 65.

[13] Smith, *Who's Afraid of Postmodernism*, 69.

suspicion" that marks our postmodern culture's relationship to Institutions of Power, including and especially the institution of the Church. Like Nietzsche, Foucault traced the lineage of secret biases and powerful prejudices that lay submerged beneath institutional truth claims, especially those ideas deemed "moral" or "normal" by institutions like Christianity. According to Foucault, nothing that is "true" is innocently and purely discovered. Instead, what those institutions (State and Religious) deem normal and moral are covertly motivated by various interests of power. It is out of this historical milieu that McLaren's Kingdom grammar has been constructed.

3

PROBLEM

What Does McLaren's
Gospel Solve?

Like four generations preceding him, McLaren defines the problem at the root of his gospel and *Kingdom* grammar differently than the historic Christian faith's conception of the problem defined by original sin. Through his protagonist Neo in his *New Kind of Christian* trilogy, McLaren contends the Christian story has been distorted, because early Christianity imported "the Greek idea of a fall from a perfect, unchanging, ideal, complete, harmonious, fully formed world into a world of change, challenge, conflict..."[1] McLaren rejects original sin; he insists there is no event of "the Fall" or corresponding "original sin" and "total depravity" in which humanity plunged into rebellion and alienation, resulting in an inherited sinful nature.[2] Instead, the framing narrative of humanity is one of systemic progression and ascent, with corresponding descent resulting in "new depths of moral evil and social injustice."[3] Accordingly, human nature has not "fallen" but is still fundamentally good,[4] progressing from an embryonic stage to a higher stage of existence. As one can see, McLaren's understanding of human nature reflects Rauschenbusch's own strong appropriation of evolutionary doctrine. As the Earth's story is one of emergence, so too is humanity's; our story is not a fall from perfection into a state of imperfection, but "unfolds as a kind of compassionate...classic coming-of-age story."[5] McLaren does

---

[1] McLaren, *The Story We Find Ourselves In*, 52. This is later affirmed and further developed in *A New Kind of Christianity*, 33-45.

[2] McLaren, *A New Kind of Christianity*, 43. In an endnote McLaren asserts that these terms "frequently derive their meaning from a story that is, I believe, inherently un-Jewish and unbiblical, and so when they are read into the biblical story, they distort and pollute it." 266n.15.

[3] McLaren, *A New Kind of Christianity*, 51.

[4] McLaren, *Story We Find Ourselves*, 52. He says, "The God-given goodness in creation isn't lost...God's creative fingerprint or signature is still there, always and forever. The evil of humanity doesn't eradicate the goodness of God's creation, even though it puts all of that goodness at risk."

[5] McLaren, *A New Kind of Christianity*, 49, 51.

not see just one single cataclysmic crisis but "an avalanche of crises."[6] As humans "come of age" they grow beyond God, and their relationship deteriorates in progressive, fitful "experiences of alienation." McLaren equates sin with "stagnation and decay," saying, "Because of this counter-emergent virus we call sin, the stages, episodes, and levels do not always unfold as they should. There are setbacks, stagnations, false starts, premature births, retardations, impatient rebellions, emergence defects, and failed attempts at emergence."[7] Sin is anti-progress, it is the opposite of the type of human progress (i.e. emergence) the Kingdom of God promotes, and for which we will see solves our human problem. What impedes human progress are bad systems and stories.

In his re-imagined framing narrative, individuals are no longer the issue, but human systems: Rather than individuals acting out of their sinful nature and sinning, "socioeconomic and technological advances" lead to moral evil and social injustice.[8] In the words of McLaren, "it's a story about the downside of 'progress'—a story of human foolishness...the

---

[6]McLaren, *The Story We Find Ourselves*, 53-54, 56. He writes, "all involve human beings gaining levels of intellectual and technological development that surpass their moral development—people becoming too smart, too powerful for their own good...Human beings leave their identity, their life, their story as creatures in God's creation...As they become more independent, they lose their connection to God, their sense of dependence...So they experience alienation from God."

[7] McLaren, *A Generous Orthodoxy*, 282.

[8] McLaren, *A New Kind of Christianity*, 51.

human turn toward rebellion...the human intention toward evil."[9] The problem is not that humans rebelled against God and are rebels or that humans did evil and are evil. For McLaren, the story is one where humans collectively create evil, damaging and savaging God's good world; it is a story where "humans have evil intent" instead of being evil themselves. Those evil intentions are not the result of an evil nature, but the bad systems and stories that consume humanity. McLaren believes the main dysfunctions of humanity are existential; he frames the crisis of the human condition as an existential crisis of prosperity, equity, and security.[10] These three crises form the "cogs" in what McLaren terms the *suicide machine*.[11]

The suicide machine is a metaphor for "the *systems* that drive our civilization toward un-health and un-peace."[12] McLaren envisions the driving force behind our broken, problematic condition to reside in the systems of the world rather than in the individual person. According to him, humanity suffers from a "dysfunction of our societal machinery," which is operated not by single individuals but by humanity acting together."[13] In other words, individual sinful human nature is not the problem, but rather a universal sin of

---

[9] McLaren, *A New Kind of Christianity*, 54.

[10] McLaren, *Everything Must Change*, 5.

[11] McLaren, *Everything Must Change*, 53.

[12] McLaren, *Everything Must Change*, 53. (emphasis mine)

[13] McLaren, *Everything Must Change*, 65.

society, which of course is how four generations of liberals defined the human problem: Rauschenbusch said sin was social, Schleiermacher and Ritschl said our problem was a kingdom or systemic "web" of sin and evil.

In *A New Kind of Christianity*, McLaren illustrates this explanation of the human condition and reality of so-called "social sin." Using the story of the Israelites in Exodus, he explains that it is a story of "liberation from the external oppression of social sin," while also celebrating "liberation from the internal spiritual oppression of personal sin."[14] Because McLaren does not believe that sin is part of human nature because of an event of rebellion, he must mean something different by "internal spiritual oppression of personal sin." It seems even this internal oppression is related to the social systems of sin, because he asserts that the Israelites were freed from "the *dominating powers* of fear, greed, impatience, ingratitude, and so on."[15] The power of Fear and Ingratitude were the oppressors, which in this Exodus narrative apparently resulted from years of being "debased by generations of slavery."[16] This slave framing story, then, is what contributed to the Israelites communal and individual commitment to "fear, greed, impatience, ingratitude, and so on." The internal compulsion toward greed, for example, was an internal power that resulted from the external system of slavery and the bad framing narrative out of which Israel was

---

[14] McLaren, *A New Kind of Christianity*, 58.

[15] McLaren, *A New Kind of Christianity*, 58. (emphasis mine.)

[16] McLaren, *A New Kind of Christianity*, 58.

liberated. Thus, our ultimate problem is bad systems and stories.

Unlike the traditional historic faith that locates the problem of the human condition in individual sinfulness and an inherited sinful nature, McLaren believes humans are in trouble because we are in bondage to the "dominant societal machinery," which entices us to keep faith in its systems of wealth, security, pleasure, and injustice.[17]   This faith and bondage has led to a sort of universal consciousness that is driven by destructive, dysfunctional framing stories. The global crises of which McLaren says we must be saved are the symptoms and consequences of the dysfunction, resulting in a collection of human evil. Dysfunctional societal machinery, destructive framing narratives, and collective human evil are our problems. Rather than sinning out of an inner, natural compulsion, innately good humans are compelled to act badly because of these environmental forces; bad systems and bad stories cause us to misbehave. Thus, we need a better system and a better story to solve for our human problem. We find both in the alternative system and story of the Kingdom which came through the person and life-work of Jesus of Nazareth.

---

[17] McLaren, *Everything Must Change*, 271.

4

SOLVER

Who is McLaren's Jesus and What Did He Do?

At the heart of liberal *Kingdom* grammar and their gospel is the person of Jesus of Nazareth, whose chief work was founding the historical movement of the Kingdom of God through His loving life example. The same is true for McLaren: The man Jesus is important because of His revolutionary Kingdom movement and model of loving life. While the historic Christian faith recognizes Jesus Christ as God and in some way a penal substitutionary sacrifice for the sins of the world, McLaren recognizes neither. Instead, Jesus is merely the best teacher of a better way of living, the one who lived the best way to be human, and one who is our best picture of the character of God. In *The Story We Find Ourselves In,* McLaren describes Jesus as a "revolutionary" who was a "master of living."[1] According to McLaren, "Jesus really is in some mysterious and in a unique way sent from God and full of God."[2] Notice McLaren does not say Jesus *is* God, but merely a messenger of sorts from God. His fellowship with God comes from His ethical way of living; Jesus is Divine because He *acts* divinely. As with four generations of liberals before him, McLaren seems to view Jesus as the moral not the metaphysical Son of God.

McLaren affirms this characterization in his most recent book, *A New Kind of Christianity,* by insisting that Jesus "brings us to a new evolutionary level in our understanding of God...the experience of God in Jesus requires a brand-new definition or understanding of God," because He "gives us the highest, deepest, and most mature view of the character of the living God."[3] McLaren's emphasis on the "character of God" finds substantial resonance with four generations of liberalism: "When you see [Jesus], you are getting the best view afforded to humans of the character of God;" "Jesus serves as the Word-made-flesh revelation of the character of God;" and "the invisible God has been made visible in his life. 'If you want to know what God is like,' Jesus says, 'look at me,

[1] McLaren, *The Story We Find Ourselves In*, 115, 121, 122.

[2] McLaren, *The Story We Find Ourselves*, 122.

[3] McLaren, *A New Kind of Christianity*, 114, 115.

my life, my ways, my deeds, my character.'"[4] Elsewhere he writes that Jesus simply identifies Himself *with* God, telling His disciples that those who had seen Him had in "some real way" also seen God.[5] In a "mysterious and unique way" Jesus is full of God. He shows, images and expresses God's character. This view of the person of Jesus is liberal in general and starkly Ritschlian in particular.

From McLaren's earliest writings one can detect his theological trajectory and emphasis of Jesus as "teacher" and "liver." In explaining Jesus as "Lord," McLaren argues this means Jesus "was the master of living...it would mean that no one else could take the raw materials of life...and elicit from them a beautiful song of truth and goodness. [The disciples] believed Jesus' way was higher and more brilliant, and the right way to launch a revolution of God."[6] Elsewhere he writes that Jesus' message and teachings is an "alternative framing story" that can "save the system from suicide," a message that focuses "on personal, social, and global transformation in this life."[7] Furthermore, "Jesus' life and message centered on the articulation and demonstration of a radically different framing story—one that critiques and exposes the imperial narratives as dangerous to itself and others."[8] The best teacher,

---

[4] McLaren, *A New Kind of Christianity*, 118, 128, 222.

[5] McLaren, *The Secret Message of Jesus*, 31.

[6] McLaren, *The Story We Find Ourselves In*, 121.

[7] McLaren, *Everything Must Change*, 73, 22.

[8] McLaren, *Everything Must Change*, 154-155.

way, and picture of God is the perfect solution to McLaren's problem, because as we already saw we need a better example to follow in order to live differently and avert dysfunction and destruction. Jesus' mastery over life through His higher, more brilliant way of living and alternative message provides the existential solution to our existential problem. Fundamentally, the solution Jesus provides through His work is the Kingdom of God, which is exactly how liberal *Kingdom* grammar has framed the solution for four generations.

Central to the work of Jesus is His vocation as the founder of the Kingdom of God, the one in whom the original way of human existence was found, taught and modeled to the world. McLaren insists that Jesus did not come to start a new religion, but to announce a new kingdom, a new way of life;[9] He was the founder of a new countermovement to all other human regimes.[10] Through His life and teachings, Jesus "inserted into human history a seed of grace, truth, and hope that can never be defeated," a seed that will "prevail over the evil and injustice of humanity and lead to the world's ongoing transformation into the world God dreams of."[11] Because the human problem is bad systems and stories, we need a new system and a new story to repair and heal us. Jesus provides humanity the solution through his teachings on the Kingdom of God and example of living out the way of that Kingdom. McLaren makes it clear that the central point of Jesus is the

[9] McLaren, *A New Kind of Christianity*, 139.

[10] McLaren, *The Secret Message of Jesus*, 66.

[11] McLaren, *Everything Must Change*, 79-80.

Kingdom of God: "[Jesus] came to launch a new Genesis, to lead a new Exodus, and to announce, embody, and inaugurate a new kingdom as the Prince of Peace. Seen in this light, Jesus and his message has everything to do with poverty, slavery, and a 'social agenda.'"[12] He insists that Jesus himself "saw these dynamics at work in his day and proposed in word and deed a new alternative. Jesus' creative and transforming framing story invited people to change the world by disbelieving old framing stories and believing a new one: a story about a loving God who calls all people to live life in a new way."[13] We are called to follow Jesus in this new way by following His teachings and example of love.

McLaren believes our problem is the dysfunctional systems and destructive stories of our world. Therefore, our solution came when God called Jesus as a messenger to show us a better way of living and teach us a better story: the Kingdom system and Kingdom story. McLaren agrees with Schleiermacher, Ritschl, Rauschenbusch and Tillich before him that the work of Jesus is fundamentally rooted in founding and living the Kingdom of God. Furthermore, Jesus is the vehicle of the Divine because of the way He lived and taught. Through His vocation as founder of the Kingdom of God Jesus was filled with God—meaning He acted like God would act on earth—and ultimately revealed the character of God by what He did and with what He said. In so acting and revealing, Jesus is the vehicle for an existential solution to our

---

[12] McLaren, *A New Kind of Christianity*, 135.

[13] McLaren, *Everything Must Change*, 237-274.

existential problem. As McLaren rhetorically asks, "Is Jesus' healing and transforming framing story really powerful enough to save the world?"[14] Because McLaren believes our systems and stories are the problem, our solution is found in an alternative system and story, which we find in Jesus' message on the Kingdom of God. McLaren answers his question thusly:

> if we believe that God graciously offers us a new way, a new truth, and a new life, we can be liberated from the vicious, addictive cycles of our suicidal framing stories. That kind of faith will save us...our failure to believe [Jesus' good news] will keep us from experiencing its saving potential, and so we'll spin on in the vicious cycles of Caesar.[15]

According to McLaren, Jesus' teachings on the Kingdom provides the liberation we need from the systems and stories of the world by providing an alternative new system and story, a new way, truth, and life. We find salvation when we "transfer our trust from the way of Caesar to the way of Christ."[16] Notice that McLaren calls people to transfer their trust to the *way* of Christ rather than *person* of Christ. McLaren urges us to transfer our trust from the world's systems and stories—from our bad *existence*—to the system and story of Christ's

---

14 McLaren, *Everything Must Change*, 269.

15 McLaren, *Everything Must Change*, 270.

16 McLaren, *Everything Must Change*, 271.

Kingdom, because the Kingdom is the actual work of Jesus. As with four generations preceding him, McLaren's *Kingdom* grammar fundamentally insists that human salvation isn't found in a *name* (i.e Jesus Christ), but a *movement*—the Kingdom of God.

5

SOLUTION

How Does McLaren's Gospel
Solve Our Problem?

In one of his clearest definitions of the Kingdom, and thus the solution to our human problem, McLaren defines the Kingdom of God as "a reality into which we have been emerging through the centuries, which is bigger than whatever we generally mean by 'Christianity' but at the same time is what generously orthodox Christianity is truly about."[1] In the same section he equates the Kingdom to "the way of

---

[1] McLaren, *A Generous Orthodoxy*, 288.

Jesus," which is "the way of love and the way of embrace."[2] The Way of Jesus and Kingdom of God "integrates what has gone before so that something new can emerge."[3] And toward what are we emerging? The universal human ideal, the essence of what it means to human: McLaren writes, "Jesus invitation into the Kingdom of God was an invitation into *the original universe, as it was meant to be.*"[4] In this definition are several features consistent with liberal *Kingdom* grammar: The Kingdom is transcendent in that it is equated with an ultimate reality that supersedes any particular religion, representing the universal ideal, the essence of human existence; it is immanent in that it is most closely embodied in humanity in the life and way of Jesus and is concerned with historical transformation; it is progressivistic in that the Kingdom takes humanity from a lower level of living to a higher level of existence; it is fundamentally about love-inspired action; finally, it is universal, in that McLaren's grammar has all of humanity squarely in view.

Like the four generations preceding McLaren, his *Kingdom* grammar is inherently defined by love-inspired action: He suggests the only way for the Kingdom of God to save humanity is through "weakness and vulnerability, sacrifice and love;"[5] McLaren argues that the central

---

[2] McLaren, *A Generous Orthodoxy*, 287.

[3] McLaren, *A Generous Orthodoxy*, 287.

[4] McLaren, *The Secret Message of Jesus*, 53. (emph. mine)

[5] McLaren, *The Secret Message of Jesus*, 69.

governing "policy" of the Kingdom is universal love;[6] he insists the way of Christ, the way of the Kingdom, is inherently the "way of love;"[7] the mission of the Church itself is defined by the single goal of "forming Christlike people, people who live the way of love, the way of peacemaking, the way of the kingdom of God, the way of Jesus;"[8] and finally, the Kingdom of God advances, gains ground "with reconciling, forgiving love: when people love strangers and enemies..."[9] This love activity flows from Jesus Himself who was the first Master at loving activity, which culminated at the cross. For McLaren, the cross is a stage upon which Christ renders a grand performance illustrating God's love, acceptance, and new Kingdom way of sacrifice and suffering. Jesus' life and message has been one of non-violence and triumph over enemies through peace and self-sacrifice. Like the other liberals, the cross is the culmination of those teachings as an exposé on love. Rather than joining in with the "'shock and awe' display of power as Roman crucifixions were intended to do," McLaren says Jesus gives us a "'reverence and awe' display of God's willingness to accept rejection and mistreatment..."[10] In this display of "Christ crucified," McLaren says "we see that the lowly way of Christ, the vulnerable way of love, is the only

---

[6] McLaren, *A New Kind of Christianity*, 154.

[7] McLaren, *A New Kind of Christianity*, 168.

[8] McLaren, *A New Kind of Christianity*, 171.

[9] McLaren, *The Secret Message of Jesus*, 69.

[10] McLaren, *A New Kind of Christianity*, 158-159.

way of life."[11] And this life is Kingdom-life. This love-inspired life is what transforms and saves humanity.

Consistent with the four previous generations of liberals, McLaren's *Kingdom* grammar is inherently progressivistic vis-à-vis humanistic change. As he says, "God stands ahead of us in time, at the end of the journey...and washes over us with a ceaseless flow of new possibilities, new options, new chances...This newness, these possibilities are always 'at hand,' 'among us,' and 'coming' so we can 'enter' the larger reality and transcend the space we currently fill." He goes on to say, "We constantly *emerge from what we were* and are into *what we can become*,"[12] equating the Kingdom of God with emergence, with humanistic progress. McLaren rhetorically asks, "What does the future hold? the answer begins, '*That depends on you and me.* God holds out to us at every moment a brighter future; the issue is whether we are willing to receive it and work with God to create it. We are participating in the creation of what the future will be.'"[13] That the future depends on you and me is patently consistent with Rauschenbusch's *social gospel*.

Along with Schleiermacher, Ritschl, and Tillich, McLaren believes that we are the makers of our best life now, we are responsible for bringing into existence the best version of ourselves, the universal human ideal; we are responsible for saving ourselves. This is the case because humanity—

---

[11] McLaren, *A New Kind of Christianity*, 169.

[12] McLaren, *A Generous Orthodoxy*, 283, 284. (emph. mine)

[13] McLaren, *A New Kind of Christianity*, 196. (emph. mine)

individuals and as a community—is the actual *medium* that contains the Kingdom of God, right here and now.[14] Furthermore, all people are called, through their own power and choice, to live in the radical new way of the Kingdom. As McLaren states, "we do indeed have the choice today and every day to seek it, enter it, receive it, live as citizens of it, invest in it, even sacrifice for it," which, depending on this choice, will create two very different worlds and futures: one hellish and one heavenly.[15] Thus, McLaren urges everyone to "start doing the next good thing now," so that the good of the Kingdom will prevail by love, peace, and endurance of suffering, while bad ethical acts like domination, violence, and torture will be overcome through our collective human effort.[16]

Ultimately, salvation is participation in the Kingdom of God, which McLaren calls participatory eschatology. While McLaren contends conventional eschatologies have cultivated resignation, fear, and aggression, participatory eschatology inspires much more:

> a passion to do good, whatever the suffering, sacrifice, and delay because of a confidence that God will win in the end; courage, because God's Spirit is at work in the world and what God begins God will surely bring to completion; a sense of urgency, because we are

---

[14] McLaren, *The Secret Message of Jesus*, 101.

[15] McLaren, *The Secret Message of Jesus*, 181.

[16] McLaren, *Everything Must Change*, 146.

> protagonists in a story; and humility and kindness, because we are aware of our ability to miss the point, lose our way, and play on the wrong side.[17]

Furthermore, McLaren argues that the death and resurrection of Jesus are paradigms for this salvation in which we ourselves are to participate in anticipation of God's coming Kingdom: we join with Jesus in dying (metaphorically to our pride and agendas, literally in martyrdom as a witness to God's Kingdom and justice); we rise again in triumph "through the mysterious but real power of God. In this cruciform way, we participate in the ongoing work of God, and we anticipate its ultimate success."[18] For McLaren, our dying and rising with Christ are symbolic of our rejection of and triumph over the dysfunctional systems and destructive stories of our world; we are called to die to the bad ethics of the world and rise to new life by living like Jesus. Thus, salvation is entirely existential, in that His loving example is what saves us from our bad existence, an existential salvation that extends to the whole human race.

In this definition of humanistic progress, we find the familiar ring of universalism present in liberal *Kingdom* grammar. McLaren believes God's wish and hope is for all of humanity to grow toward Christlikeness, because we are *all* children of God.[19] In fact, McLaren believes that "a person can

---

[17] McLaren, *A New Kind of Christianity*, 200.

[18] McLaren, *A New Kind of Christianity*, 200-201.

[19] McLaren, *A Generous Orthodoxy*, 283.

affiliate with Jesus in the kingdom-of-God dimension without affiliating with him in the religious kingdom of Christianity. In other words, I believe that Christianity is not the kingdom of God. The ultimate reality is the kingdom of God..."[20] Because the Christian faith is not the single container of God's reign, the Kingdom is universal; it is a universal human ideal instantiated in the person and life of Jesus whom all may join simply by emulating Him.

McLaren insists that everyone is a potential agent of the Kingdom by nature of people's loving activity, like the taxi cab driver McLaren references who treated his guests with special care and respect; Carter had within him the spirit of the Kingdom of God and was a secret agent of the Kingdom.[21] For McLaren this can be true because the Kingdom is about our daily lives, it is a daily way of life centered around Jesus' loving message and life example. He stresses the Kingdom is about so-called *purposeful inclusion*, because it "seeks to include all who want to participate in and contribute to its purpose,"[22] which of course is humanistic progress toward bringing the universal human ideal—in McLaren's words, the original universe as it was meant to be—to bear on human existence.

Consequently, McLaren finds it "fascinating" to think that thousands of Muslims, Buddhists, Hindus, and even former atheists and agnostics could come from the east and west and

---

[20] McLaren, *A Generous Orthodoxy*, 282n.141.

[21] McLaren, *The Secret Message of Jesus*, 85-89.

[22] McLaren, *The Secret Message of Jesus*, 167.

north and south "to enjoy the feast of the kingdom in ways that those bearing the name Christian have not."[23] McLaren would believe this possible because he believes that anything that contributes to humanistic progress counts as Kingdom activity; any loving-act that subverts the prevailing systems and stories solves for our human problem and provides individual salvation.

In the end, because we are called to live in the system and story of the Kingdom by living the teachings of Jesus, McLaren says ultimate salvation at judgment will be based on behavior, not beliefs: "God will examine the story of our lives for signs of Christlikeness...These are the parts of a person's life that will be deemed worthy of being saved, remembered, rewarded, and raised to new beginnings."[24] Giving food and water to the needy, showing mercy, welcoming the stranger, and being generous like Jesus is what God cares about, what will result in salvation. Conversely, "all the unloving, unjust, non-Christlike parts of our lives...will be burned away, counted as unworthy, condemned, and forgotten forever."[25]

Notice the implicit universalism embedded in McLaren's soteriology: in the end, everyone will find salvation, because, as Tillich taught, the positive will live on while the negative will not. Ultimately, then, our salvation depends upon our *existence*, it depends upon how we live, whether we walked the path of Jesus in word, deed, and suffering. Since "no good

---

[23] McLaren, *The Secret Message of Jesus*, 217.

[24] McLaren, *A New Kind of Christianity*, 204.

[25] McLaren, *A New Kind of Christianity*, 204.

deed will be forgotten," we are urged to "start doing the next good thing now and never give up until the dream comes true," until God's Kingdom comes.[26] Therefore, in reality, salvation comes not through *Jesus'* saving act on the cross, but through every *human* act that lives out Jesus' way of life. In many ways, each person is his own savior, because every act of love counts as Kingdom acts, as saving acts that bring the universal ideal to bear on existence. In reality, the *Kingdom* saves us through humanistic progress, rather than through Jesus.

---

[26] McLaren, *Everything Must Change*, 146.

The Gospel of Brian McLaren

6

CONCLUSION

This *Kingdom* salvation of which McLaren speaks is wholly consistent with four generations of liberal *Kingdom* grammar and the liberal gospel itself. In this *grammar*, our human problem is not a sinful nature but dysfunctional systems and destructive stories. Rather than bound by sin on the inside, we are oppressed on the outside by bad social and spiritual systems and stories. Jesus is the antidote, the cure for these bad systems and stories because He provided the alternative system and story of the Kingdom through His life and teachings. For McLaren, the Kingdom of God is "A life that is radically different from the way people are living these days, a life that is full and over flowing, a higher life that is centered in an interactive relationship with God and with Jesus...an extraordinary life to the full centered on a relationship with God."[1] He contends this is what the Apostle John termed "eternal life," or "life of the ages." Through his Kingdom message and Kingdom way of living, "Jesus is promising a life that transcends 'life in the present age'...[he] is offering a life in the new Genesis, the new creation that is 'of the age' not simply part of the current regimes, plots, kingdoms, and economies created by humans."[2]

At the heart of McLaren's gospel is a person named Jesus who came to liberate us from these old regimes (i.e. dysfunctional systems) and plots (i.e. destructive stories), to teach and show us the highest, best way found in the Kingdom. He came to end *life-as-we-know-it* and usher in *life-as-it-ought-to-be*; Jesus' life saves, rather than His death and resurrection. This essence of what it means to be human is rooted in universal brotherly love. The Kingdom represents this ultimate reality, which comes when anyone does any act of love, whether cleaning a local river, launching an adult literacy program, or returning a dropped set of keys to a stranger on a busy city sidewalk. Somehow these love-inspired acts collectively bring in the future we all long for, burning up the negative in the process and enveloping all of humanity in its arms of inclusion. And in the end, while Jesus' life provides the example and way, humanity is its own savior. That is the

---

[1] McLaren, *The Secret Message of Jesus*, 37.

[2] McLaren, *A New Kind of Christianity*, 130.

obvious, logical conclusion to liberal *Kingdom* grammar, which McLaren recites *in toto*.

In the end, the gospel of Brian McLaren is identical with the good news of liberalism: the Kingdom of God, the universal human ideal and essence of human existence, has come near in the life of Jesus; live your best existence now by turning from the destructive stories and dysfunctional systems of this world and turning toward everyday acts of brotherly love. We conclude this examination by considering an observation and a few implications that contemporary appropriations of liberal gospel of the Kingdom are already having within evangelicalism.

First, an observation: in tracing the generational development of liberal Kingdom grammar it is interesting to note the ways in which the focus on the Church itself shifted and waned. When Schleiermacher introduced the language of the Kingdom back into the Church's theological discourse, the Church was squarely in view: He equated the Kingdom with the Church. Ritschl maintained such a connection, yet broadened the Kingdom to include those well beyond its borders. By the time Tillich formulated his own theological enterprise, the Church had become a symbol and mostly unnecessary.

Likewise, in McLaren's theological missive arguing for a new kind of Christianity, the Church is roundly ignored in favor of the Kingdom as the ultimate religious reality. This gradual downplaying and dismissal of the Church makes sense, as the Church is simply one faith community that embodies the universal human ideal and is important only insofar as it was the original religious organization that perpetuated Jesus' teachings. Now in our postmodern multi-faith world, there is even more pressure to downplay and negate the role of the Church as the particular embodiment of Christ and agent of the Kingdom. Such maneuvers have two implications for the future of mainstream evangelicalism.

First, note how the terms *mission, evangelism,* and *gospel* seem to have shifted over the past few years in light of the resurgent use of the Kingdom of God. While perhaps the nature of Jesus and His substitutionary work on the cross is not in danger of losing their meaning and significance in such circles, one has to wonder how using the Kingdom in ways liberals have for generations will begin to affect mainstream evangelical commitment to core evangelical convictions, mainly conversionism and activism—particularly evangelistic. Popular Evangelical magazines such as *RELEVANT,* books on Christian cultural engagement such as *AND: The Gathered and Scattered Church*[3] and *For the City: Proclaiming and Living Out the Gospel,*[4] and young church leader conferences like *Catalyst* emphasize doing good by living like Jesus. Not that this emphasis is necessarily a bad thing. It seems, however, that in so emphasizing the Kingdom in ways that liberals have for years—mainly transforming human existence through mundane and supramundane acts of love—mainstream

---

[3] Hugh Halter and Matt Smay, *AND: The Gathered and Scattered Church* (Grand Rapids: Zondervan, 2010).

[4] Darin Patrick and Matt Carter, *For the City: Proclaiming and Living Out the Gospel* (Grand Rapids: Zondervan, 2010).

evangelicals are in danger of losing sight of what has always been central to evangelicalism, and authentic, historic Christianity.

Furthermore, evangelicals should think twice about appropriating the grammar of the Kingdom in ways liberals have because of the implications that grammar has for the Christian faith itself. How liberals like McLaren arrive at their definition of *Kingdom* depends on how they define sin, the person and work of Jesus, and other aspects of historic orthodoxy. In light of that grammar, then, what is to say mainstream evangelicals will not join progressives in transforming, say, the meaning of the cross itself? Already McLaren has accused proponents of substitutionary atonement of holding a view akin to "divine child abuse."[5] And while others do not go as far as this language they wonder whether we should speak of the cross in language that side-steps traditional substitutionary language altogether in favor of alternative atonement views, such as *Christus Victor*.

What is to stop mainstream evangelicals from joining McLaren in downplaying the significance of Jesus' death in favor of Jesus' significant life? Perhaps more importantly, if the deeds and teachings of Jesus are all that matter, then what would stop some evangelicals from fudging on the *person* of Jesus, including His deity? Without sounding apocalyptic, if evangelicals continue to use the language of the Kingdom in ways that liberals have for generations, they risk the potential of joining them in the other beliefs that supplied the context

---

[5] McLaren, *The Story We Find Ourselves*, 102.

and definition of that grammar. So the first implication in adopting liberal *Kingdom* grammar is the danger of losing sight of the historic Christian faith.

Secondly, the Kingdom gospel of liberals and Emergent's like McLaren has massive implications for the future of missions and evangelism. A new generation is thinking differently about the nature of evangelism at home and missions abroad. For instance, in times past the typical evangelical college would take students on Spring Break trips to key beaches around the country to share the gospel with Spring Break revelers. While such methods of evangelism could be contested, it is worth noting that now it is more common for such colleges to take trips to serve the homeless in Seattle or build wells in Africa than it is to share the gospel with people in need of a Savior. Missions is now about acts of love in the interest of serving our neighbor, rather than acts of gospel proclamation in the interest of seeing our neighbor saved. Furthermore, alongside a shift in emphasis in missions has been a shift in evangelism, the hallmark of mission work of yore. Rather than evangelism being the proclamation of the gospel, people now define evangelism using the maxim often ascribed to St. Francis of Assisi: preach the gospel at all times, if necessary use words. Words that urge repentance, belief, and confession are considered unnecessary, being abandoned in favor of actions of acceptance, service, and love.

People like McLaren now frame the gospel as the Kingdom coming to our here-and-now rather than justification by faith in Christ. While the Kingdom is part and parcel of the gospel of Jesus Christ, McLaren is pronouncing at the expense of the justification provided through Jesus' death and resurrection. Such pronouncement not only has implications for the future of mission and evangelism, but the gospel itself. Therefore, it behooves evangelicals to reconsider their *Kingdom* grammar in order to guard their *gospel* grammar. Yes, we must pray for God's Kingdom-rule to break into our existence in increasing measure. But we do so with the realization that it was God Himself through His Son's life, death, and resurrection that made it possible in the first place. It is not the *Kingdom* that saves us, but Jesus Christ alone.

The Gospel of Brian McLaren

PART 2

A New Kind of Christianity for a Multi-Faith World

The Gospel of Brian McLaren

7

INTRODUCTION

Brian McLaren reminds me a lot of Thomas Jefferson: He conveniently ignores large portions of the Holy Scripture that do not conform to His worldview.

Jefferson is known to have cobbled together a Bible that cut out the miracles of Jesus and supernatural elements of the Gospels, because they didn't conform to his modern, Enlightenment worldview. Similarly, in his newest book, *Why Did Jesus, Moses, the Buddha, and Mohammed Cross the Road?: Christian Identity in a Multi-Faith World*, McLaren has ignored entire portions of the Bible that don't conform to his postmodern, pluralism worldview.

He has ignored the Lord's command to Israel to not worship any other God but YHWH. He has ignored the anger and judgement of God over Israel's pervasive pattern of idolatry throughout the Old Testament. He has ignored the New Testament's teachings that Jesus Christ Himself is the only one true God. He has ignored Scripture's teachings on salvation by grace through faith in Jesus Christ alone.

Like Jefferson, McLaren has conveniently ignored the Bible in favor of a Christian religious identity that isn't actually Christian. Instead, it is fundamentally foreign to the Holy Scripture and historic Christian faith.

Now understand, I am not arguing McLaren *himself* is not a Christian. That's not for me to decide; God holds final judgment in that regard. What I am arguing in Part 2 of our examination of *The Gospel of Brian McLaren* is that his *ideas* are not Christian. In addition to examining his view of our human problem, the solution to our problem, and the bearer of our solution, this final section outlining McLaren's postmodern, pluralism worldview will show that his gospel is no gospel at all. His gospel is fake, because he ignores the Bible and fundamentals of the Christian faith.

McLaren's gospel hinges on his desire to develop "a healthy, sane and faithful Christian identity in a multi-faith world."[1] This is an admirable desire. Given our multi-faith reality, finding a way to get along and exist as Christians alongside people of other faiths is indeed needed. But the way

---

[1] Brian McLaren, *Why Did Jesus, Moses, the Buddha, and Mohammed Cross the Road? Christian Identity in a Multi-Faith World* (New York: Jericho Books, 2012), 9.

McLaren goes about it is faulty, as he has no regard for the exclusivity of faith in Jesus Christ as single Lord and Savior. Instead, he wants to develop a Christian religious identity "that moves me toward people of other faiths in wholehearted love, not in spit of their non-Christian identity and not in spite or my own Christian identity, but *because of my identity as a follower of God in the way of Jesus.*"[2] Notice that McLaren isn't a follower of Jesus, but instead a follower of God in the *way* of Jesus. This distinction is crucial, because this descriptive nuance broadens the solution to our problem well beyond Jesus Christ and into religious pluralism in ways others have argued for years. For McLaren, the point is following God—a vanilla, pan-deity that stands as the Higher Being of all religious faiths—and Jesus is merely one way among many possible ways to follow.

While the Christian gospel insists that salvation is found in no one other than Jesus Christ, McLaren's gospel insists that something good shines from the heart of all religions, which is "a saving drive toward peace, goodness, self-control, integrity, charity, beauty, duty."[3] McLaren is on mission to rethink Christian identity in a multi-faith world, and in so doing he completely redefines and reimagines the Christian faith itself.

This second part of Brian McLaren's gospel will explain how he reimagines Christian religious identity, reformulates

---

[2] McLaren, *Jesus, Moses, the Buddha, and Mohammed*, 11. (emph. mine)

[3] McLaren, *Jesus, Moses, the Buddha, and Mohammed*, 20.

key doctrines of the Christian faith, reconstructs important Church practices, and redefines Christian mission. While McLaren's latest enterprise is indeed sad, it shouldn't surprise anyone because it is a firm extension of the generational enterprise of theological liberalism. This iteration is the logical extension of the liberal gospel for a postmodern day.

As I read McLaren's newest book I couldn't help but think about Paul's journey to Athens recorded in Acts 17. For longtime Christians it's a well-known story in which Paul encounters a marketplace "full of idols" in Athens, much like our own multi-faith day in America. How does Paul respond? First, he follows McLaren's cues in moving toward people of other faiths "in wholehearted love" by acknowledging and appreciating their religiosity. But unlike McLaren, he carries that love further, beyond mere tolerance, to confronting these religious people with the only one true God of the Holy Scriptures. After calling them "ignorant," Paul goes on to tell the Story of this God. He then boldly, courageously calls these idolaters out from their ignorance by repenting, saying that "In the past God overlooked such ignorance, but now He commands people everywhere to repent," (Acts 17:30) to repent of their false worship of false gods. In fact, God "has set a day when He will judge the world" (Acts 17:31) for the very ignorant idolatry that McLaren champions! Unlike the apology McLaren has written, what we see here in Acts 17 is the only posture the Church has ever taken toward other faiths, and it is one that's especially important for Christian identity in a multi-faith world.

So, according to McLaren, why did Jesus, Moses, the Buddha, and Mohammed cross the road? "Because they hoped we would follow them."[4] McLaren's gospel truly sketches a brand new kind of Christianity for a multi-faith world, which isn't good news for anyone.

---

[4] McLaren, *Jesus, Moses, the Buddha, and Mohammed*, 12.

The Gospel of Brian McLaren

8

REIMAGINING CHRISTIAN IDENTITY

The singular goal of McLaren's book is to rethink Christian identity in a multi-faith world. In so rethinking, McLaren insists that we (mostly conservative evangelical Christians, McLaren's favorite whipping boy) need a strong-benevolent Christian identity, a so-called "third way" Christian identity that is both strong—"vigorous, vital, durable, motivating, faithful, attractive, and defining" [1] —and kind—"something far more robust than mere tolerance,

---

[1] McLaren, *Jesus, Moses, the Buddha, and Mohammed*, 10.

political correctness, or coexistence," and instead "benevolent, hospitable, accepting, interested, and loving...seeking to understand and appreciate their religion from their point of view."[2] He writes on this issue of Christian religious identity from his own personal experience with a problematic syndrome he calls CRIS.

McLaren insists Christians like him have a problem: They suffer from so-called "Conflicted Religious Identity Syndrome (CRIS)." This condition afflicts people like him who are "seeking a way of being Christian that makes you more hospitable, not more hostile...more loving, not more judgmental...more like Christ and less like many churchgoers you have met."[3] The word *hostile* plays an important role in McLaren's argument for reimagining Christian religious identity in a multi-faith world, as it allows him to pit hospitable Christians like him against so-called hostile Christians like conservative evangelicals.

Key to McLaren's reimagining efforts is painting conservative Christians, who care that their non-Christian neighbors place their faith in Jesus Christ, as having "a strong identity characterized by strong hostility toward non-christians."[4] He contends that such an identity, rooted in hostility and oppositionalism, "values us as inherently more human, more holy, more acceptable, more pure, or more

[2] McLaren, *Jesus, Moses, the Buddha, and Mohammed*, 10-11.

[3] McLaren, *Jesus, Moses, the Buddha, and Mohammed*, 15.

[4] McLaren, *Jesus, Moses, the Buddha, and Mohammed*, 41.

worthy than them...Our root problem is the hostility that we often employ to make and keep our identities strong."[5] Thus, McLaren is pleading with traditional Christians to become less hostile,[6] to leave behind "an oppositional religious identity that derives strength from hostility."[7] *Religious hostility* is a potent rhetorical device that McLaren uses throughout to paint his opponents as hateful monsters. It is derived, however, from an unfair caricature of fair-minded, concerned Christians who long for their friends and neighbors of other religions to find salvation through Jesus Christ, which the Bible and Church have insisted on for two millennia.

In response to the hostility of traditional Christians, McLaren argues for a different posture: He wants them to replace their hostility with *solidarity*, which he urges in the final of ten questions testing ones Christian identity:

> "My understanding of Jesus and his message leads me to see each faith tradition, including my own, as having its own history, value, strengths, and weaknesses. I seek to affirm and celebrate all that is good in each faith tradition, and I build intentional relationships of mutual sharing and respectful collaboration with people of all faith traditions, so all our faiths can keep growing and

---

[5] McLaren, *Jesus, Moses, the Buddha, and Mohammed*, 63.

[6] McLaren, *Jesus, Moses, the Buddha, and Mohammed*, 44.

[7] McLaren, *Jesus, Moses, the Buddha, and Mohammed*, 57.

contributing to God's will being done on earth as in heaven."[8]

Note several assumptions in this push for solidarity: Christianity is simply one faith option among several legitimate "faith communities;" every religious tradition is good and legitimate; Jesus Himself and His message apparently leads us to affirm and celebrate the good in other religions; every religion contributes to God's will unfolding on earth, every faith contributes to the Kingdom of God advancing. McLaren insists it is possible to accept people of other faiths "with the religion they love,"[9] because there is something good that shines in every religion.

Not only is McLaren's main thesis problematic from the perspective of Scripture—the Bible is clear there is only one true God, Jesus Christ, and all else are false gods[10]—it is problematic in that his starting place of *Christian identity* is a false definition of our position in the first place. We are not interested in converting people from one religious identity to our Christian identity, from another religion to Christianity, as McLaren claims.[11] The Church's mission has always been to help and provoke people to give their life and lifestyle to Jesus Christ as Lord and Rescuer, to place their faith in Him. Christianity or a Christian religious identity have never been

---

[8] McLaren, *Jesus, Moses, the Buddha, and Mohammed*, 69.

[9] McLaren, *Jesus, Moses, the Buddha, and Mohammed*, 32.

[10] See 1 Cor. 8:4-6.

[11] McLaren, *Jesus, Moses, the Buddha, and Mohammed*, 31.

the point. Jesus is the point. And faith in Him as Lord and Savior and everything that comes along with that faith— release from the bondage of sin, freedom from the oppression of shame and guilt, salvation from death— is the point. Again, Christianity has never been the point. Jesus Christ as the only one true God who is humanity's only hope for rescue is.

Furthermore, McLaren's assumptions regarding Christian identity also play into his broader views of religion. It seems clear that he believes every religion, or every so-called "faith tradition," is valid, legitimate, and good. Every faith has strengths and every faith has weaknesses. Thus, McLaren calls on traditional Christians to shed our hostile identity and instead walk in solidarity with our fellow brothers and sisters in faith—regardless of the particulars of that faith. But here's the problem, well several problems, actually: McLaren's optimistic, rosy-glass view of religious harmony is misguided; religion itself is a social construct; the whole Holy Scriptures make clear there is only one true God, and all other gods are false; and there is one way to become right with that one true God.

First, McLaren's rosy-glass view of religious harmony is misguided because every religion makes exclusive claims. I found it remarkable that McLaren seemed to downplay and even dismiss the reality that every religion makes exclusive claims, ones that tend to negate other religious claims. This is Comparative Religion 101, here. Islam declares there is only one God, Allah, and Muhammad is his messenger, implying that beliefs about all other claims to deity, like those by Christians about Jesus, are false. In fact, Muslims make the explicit claim that Jesus is merely one prophet among many, beginning with Adam, the first Muslim, and ending with Muhammed who was the last and greatest. Buddhism is complicated because of its history, but generally Buddhists have a view of God among other things, that conflicts with monotheists, or even polytheists. Though they don't deny the existence of God, or multiple gods, per se, for Buddhists whether there are gods doesn't matter because they have nothing to say about ultimate existence; only the Buddha has revealed the way beyond this existence into a higher existence. In Islam and Buddhism alone, McLaren's thesis is negated, as oppositionalism—and, we could say, *hostility*—is built into these religions by nature of their own exclusive worldview claims.

Second, religion itself is a social construct. It is a way social beings organize themselves around a particular reality defining story—and subsequent beliefs regarding that story—in response to some religious affection. The idea that multiple religions exist is true insofar as humans themselves in socially coordinated efforts have constructed belief systems in response to what theological liberals have called a "feeling of absolute dependence," or a feeling of dependence on a Higher Being. Such human affection and feeling does not validate a particular religious experience, only revelation can do that. Paul makes clear in Romans 1 that countless human societies know the only one true God, yet they've exchanged Him for "images," for socially constructed religions.

In the Bible these social constructs were known as Baal or Asherah of the Canaanites, the god Pharaoh of Egypt, or the "unknown god" of the Athenians. In our modern, multi-faith world these social constructs are known as Allah or Buddha or Krishna. The only true revelation humans have ever had regarding a "Higher Being" is the Holy Scripture, which reveals a very particular God: Jesus Christ. And that revelation insists that faith in Him is the only "religious" experience that is real, while all other experiences we define as religious are fake.

Third, as previously mentioned, the Bible makes it clear that there is only one true God. The church has always understood that one true God as Trinity—Father, Son, and Spirit. This does not mean God is three gods in one, but rather three persons with one essence. This God is not the same god worshiped by Islam, Buddhism, or even Judaism. And any attempt to blur the distinction between these fake gods and the only one true God of the Bible is nothing short of idolatry. The *Shema* of Deuteronomy makes this clear: "Hear, O Israel. The Lord our God, the Lord is One." And Paul does, too, when he address a situation in the Church of Corinth with food sacrificed to idols. He quotes the *Shema* and then amends it, saying:

> "We know that 'An idol is nothing at all in the world' and that 'There is no God but one.' For even if there are so-called gods, whether in heaven or on earth (as indeed there are many 'gods' and many 'lords'), yet for us there is but one God, the Father, from whom all things came and for whom we live; and there is but one Lord, Jesus Christ, through whom all things came and through whom we live." (I Cor 8)

Here Paul makes clear that Jesus Christ is the only one true God. The 'gods' and 'lords' of this world are mere social constructs, created by people in place of the true God.

Finally, the only revelation we've received from God Himself makes it clear there is one way to become right with this God: Rescue by grace through faith in Jesus. There is no other name under heaven by which a person can be saved (Acts 4). No one comes to the God the Father except through God the Son (John 14). There is but one God, the Father; there is but one Lord, Jesus Christ, through whom all things came and through whom we live (1 Cor 8). Everybody is made right with God by His grace through the rescue that's come by Christ Jesus, whom God presented as a sacrifice of atonement, to be received by faith (Romans 3). To teach anything else is false teaching; to suggest the Holy Scriptures teach anything else is heresy.

It would be bad enough if McLaren stopped his enterprise here at reimagining Christian identity, but he doesn't. He takes it a step further by insisting we need to reformulate Christian doctrine itself.

9

REFORMULATING CHRISTIAN DOCTRINE

In many ways McLaren's doctrine reformulation is rooted in his reformulation of two foundational doctrines of the historic Christian faith: Scripture and God. According to McLaren, the Bible isn't to be read and interpreted and applied like some do as a constitution, as if it was an absolute authority on everything in life.[1] In *A New Kind of Christianity*, McLaren couldn't (bring himself to) say that the Bible is inspired by God and is the sole textual point of God's divine self-disclosure, only that it has "a unique role in the life of the

---

[1] McLaren, *Jesus, Moses, the Buddha, and Mohammed*, 204.

community of faith, resourcing, challenging, and guiding the community of faith in ways that no other texts can."[2] How, then, does McLaren conceive of the Bible as an authoritative document? The Bible is a community library.

For him "the Bible is a library filled with diverse voices making diverse claims in an ongoing conversation."[3] As he maintained in *A New Kind of Christianity*, "This inspired library preserves, presents, and inspires an ongoing vigorous conversation with and about God, a living and vital civil argument into which we are all invited and through which God is revealed."[4] A fuller quotation from the same book illumines his view of Scripture and its authority more clearly:

> "[Revelation] happens in conversations and arguments that take place within and among communities of people who share the same essential questions across generations. Revelation accumulates in the relationships, interactions, and interplay between statements."[5]

Pay attention to what he is saying here: McLaren believes revelation is about *human conversation* about God, rather than God Himself revealing Himself to humanity. This is why he can say in this recent book, "Faithful interaction with a library means siding with some of those voices and against

---

2 McLaren, *A New Kind of Christianity*, 83.

3 McLaren, *Jesus, Moses, the Buddha, and Mohammed*, 204.

4 McLaren, *A New Kind of Christianity*, 83.

5 McLaren, *A New Kind of Christianity*, 91-92.

others."[6] In fact, reimagining our Christian identity in a multi-faith world "requires us to go back and reread our Scriptures and 'flip them,' faithfully picking and choosing—subverting hostility in the strong pursuit of love."[7]

And how can McLaren suggest this? Because Paul himself faithfully picked and chose, or that's what he would lead us to believe. McLaren argues that Paul edits two passages of Scripture in the Old Testament—Psalm 18:41-49 and Deuteronomy 32:43—to reimagine salvation in Romans 15:8-10. Remarkably, McLaren suggests that "Paul courageously re-articulated the meaning of salvation,"[8] which he says was inspired by Jesus himself,[9] as if both of them were simply adding their voices to an ongoing conversation about God's salvation movement. It seems clear McLaren doesn't believe God Himself is actually saying something through the Bible, merely that people are trying to say something about God. And we are called to carry forth this "picking and choosing" effort to say something more advanced and more magnanimous than other people have said, including people in Scripture. McLaren says this very thing when he writes, "It remains to be seen to what degree we Christians today will move forward with Jesus and to what degree we will dig our

---

[6] McLaren, *Jesus, Moses, the Buddha, and Mohammed*, 204.

[7] McLaren, *Jesus, Moses, the Buddha, and Mohammed*, 203.

[8] McLaren, *Jesus, Moses, the Buddha, and Mohammed*, 203.

[9] McLaren, *Jesus, Moses, the Buddha, and Mohammed*, 202.

heels in with the less magnanimous voices in the biblical library."[10]

I'd sure be interested to know what "less magnanimous voices in the biblical library" he's referencing. And if we can simply "side with some voices and against others" because they don't conform to our current, contemporary conversations about God, how isn't this precisely "simply picking and choosing according to one's own tastes," which McLaren denies? While I acknowledge a careful, deliberate interpretive effort surrounds our interaction with the text, it seems clear that for McLaren meaning doesn't reside in the text itself, because God Himself isn't speaking. Instead, the interpreter decides by way of siding and opposing what the Bible says, or perhaps more accurately, *should* say in light of our 21st century God-conversation. This makes more sense when one understands McLaren's understanding of God.

Interestingly, McLaren's understanding of God seems to mirror the view of tritheism. Tritheism is the view of God that emphasizes the three persons of the Godhead with little to no unity of essence. It denies the essential unity of the Trinity in favor of three separate Gods, which is contrary to the historic Christian faith. Brian seems to reject the way in which historic orthodoxy has understood the Trinity for centuries. In fact, McLaren actually suggests that the doctrine of the Trinity is responsible for anti-semitism,[11] the Nazi gas chambers,[12] is no

---

[10] McLaren, *Jesus, Moses, the Buddha, and Mohammed*, 206.

[11] McLaren, *Jesus, Moses, the Buddha, and Mohammed*, 126.

[12] McLaren, *Jesus, Moses, the Buddha, and Mohammed*, 126.

more than a "sinister tool of mind and speech control,"[13] and has threatened Muslims, Hindus, Buddhists, and members of indigenous religions.[14] You may think I am unfairly representing McLaren's position here. Unfortunately, I am not for he says "Trinitarian doctrines have indeed been part of the problem."[15] While the Trinity has been central to the Christian faith from the beginning—mainly because of what it says about Jesus Christ specifically as much as it says about God generally—McLaren seems to mock its centrality and importance to the Church.[16] How, then, does McLaren conceive of God, particularly in his reimagined Trinity?

Of the Trinity McLaren says, "God is one and in *some sense* three; that Christ is man and in *some sense* God; that the Spirit is the Spirit of the Father and the Son but in *some sense* not reducible to the Father and the Son."[17] I'm not sure why McLaren uses the qualifier "in some sense" to describe the Trinity, especially Jesus. The historic Christian faith has always said that God is one essence *and* three persons (curiously, McLaren leaves "*essence*" out of his concept of God, which makes more sense below); that Jesus Christ is man *and* God;

---

[13] McLaren, *Jesus, Moses, the Buddha, and Mohammed*, 128.

[14] McLaren, *Jesus, Moses, the Buddha, and Mohammed*, 126.

[15] McLaren, *Jesus, Moses, the Buddha, and Mohammed*, 127.

[16] McLaren, *Jesus, Moses, the Buddha, and Mohammed*, 127.

[17] McLaren, *Jesus, Moses, the Buddha, and Mohammed*, 127. (emph. mine)

THE GOSPEL OF BRIAN MCLAREN

that the Holy Spirit is a separate Being, yet one with the Father and the Son—not merely *in some sense*, but actually so.

McLaren rejects the historical (i.e. Nicene) understanding of the Trinity in favor of so-called *Social Trinitarianism*, a view he claims is supported by church history, particularly the Cappadocian Fathers.[18] Without going into great detail here given the scope of this examination, McLaren's assumptions regarding the Cappadocian Fathers are dependent upon problematic readings of their works.[19] And because McLaren relies upon Jurgen Moltmann's trinitarian scheme—who called his own view "trinitarian panentheism"—we see an emphasis on the three persons of God at the expense of his essential unity; McLaren's view is similar to the heresy of tritheism.

Like other social trinitarians, McLaren "images God as a dynamic unity-in-community of self-giving persons-in-relationship."[20] In this view, Father, Son, and Spirit are neither three independent units bound into a larger unity, nor one independent unit with three identical parts.[21] According to McLaren, God is the relational unity in which each person of

---

[18] McLaren, *Jesus, Moses, the Buddha, and Mohammed*, 128.

[19] For an excellent treatment of the Trinity, especially in regards to religious pluralism, see Keith E. Johnson, *Rethinking the Trinity and Religious Pluralism: An Augustinian Assessment* (Downers Grove: IVP Academic, 2011).

[20] McLaren, *Jesus, Moses, the Buddha, and Mohammed*, 128.

[21] McLaren, *Jesus, Moses, the Buddha, and Mohammed*, 128.

the Trinity relate.[22]   Rather than God being defined as an essential unity of three persons, as historic Nicene Christianity has always defined God, McLaren's conception of the Trinity makes God out to be a *community* rather than an *essential unity*. Thus, for McLaren, the "triune God" is merely the community of divine beings, which verges on the heresy of tritheism.

While McLaren does use the Eastern Church's view of *perichoresis* (mutual indwelling) to bind Father-Son-Spirit together, like Moltmann he fails to recognize how united the East and West were in their view of the unity of the Godhead in *essence*, in nature. And instead of conceiving of this mutual indwelling as governing their essential unity as three persons, McLaren merely projects a human scheme of ideal social relatedness upon the Godhead. Theology, then, very quickly mirrors anthropology, in that humanism defines and governs theism. In the historic view of the Godhead, however, it isn't that God functions like some human community of love, where the persons of the Trinity are bound together by such love in community and thus form the Being of God. Instead, God is defined as one essential Being who knows, wills, and acts in concert as three persons, yet as one Being. This is not McLaren's understanding of God.

It is problematic that McLaren views God merely as a human community of persons without having a strong belief in their essential unity of nature. It's a problem primarily because Jesus Christ is left as merely a person who exhibits the

---

[22] McLaren, *Jesus, Moses, the Buddha, and Mohammed*, 128.

character of love. If Jesus is not united in essence with the Father as God, then He isn't God Himself. If the Holy Spirit isn't united in essence with the Father and Son, then he can act separately, particularly in other religions which McLaren affirms.[23] Because the Holy Spirit isn't bound in essential unity to the Father and Son, "we would expect the one Holy Spirit to be moving, working, 'hovering' over each religion" as McLaren argues.[24] More bizarrely, McLaren seems to suggest all people actually participate in this divine community as *interpersons* or *interpersonalities*, because we are creatures made in God's image.[25] Thus, every religious community encounters God equally, because all people share in the divine community—"we live, move, and have our being in the Spirit" and "each religion...[has] a unique, particular, and evolving perspective from which to encounter the Spirit in a unique way."[26] It is for this reasons McLaren's understanding of God is suspect and should be roundly rejected.

The danger in projecting humanistic social relatedness upon God—as merely a community of persons, while the essential unity of Father-Son-Spirit in nature is ignored—comes to the surface when one realizes religious pluralists use such a view to argue for God's different saving activities among other religious communities. We see such an advocacy

---

[23] McLaren, *Jesus, Moses, the Buddha, and Mohammed*, 153.

[24] McLaren, *Jesus, Moses, the Buddha, and Mohammed*, 153.

[25] McLaren, *Jesus, Moses, the Buddha, and Mohammed*, 129.

[26] McLaren, *Jesus, Moses, the Buddha, and Mohammed*, 152.

when examining the rest of McLaren's gospel scheme, which includes our problem and human identity; the saving solution to our problem; and the one who bore our solution, Jesus.

McLaren's gospel for a multi-faith world begins at the beginning with creation, moving from there to the doctrine of sin. I will not rehash here what I did in chapter 3 regarding our problem, except to say that it is important to realize that McLaren believes that people still exist in their original goodness. While he rightly insists that every person shares the same divine image and are created in the image of God,[27] he wrongly assumes that original good image is still intact and unaffected by original sin. As he argues, "We are trusting that original sin, for all its terrifying power, is not more powerful than the more original goodness God has written into the code of creation and of us."[28] McLaren's belief that God's original goodness is still written into the our code and creation's code reflects the 5th century heresy known as Pelagianism.

Pelagianism is named after Pelagius, a British monk who later moved to Rome and was made famous for his heated exchanges with another famous Christian thinker: Augustine. Pelagius believed that the original spark of divine goodness was still present in humanity, that we are not fundamentally cracked and broken image bearers as Augustine and other early church fathers believed. If we are still by-nature intact image bearers of God, why do we sin? Four reasons:

---

[27] McLaren, *Jesus, Moses, the Buddha, and Mohammed*, 103.

[28] McLaren, *Jesus, Moses, the Buddha, and Mohammed*, 159.

Ignorance; bad examples, which lead to bad habits; and habits that perpetuate into continued patterns and systems of sin. Pelagius believed that people were capable of choosing, on their own, either good actions or bad actions. Accordingly, nature does not compel a person to sin; ignorance, examples, habits, and systemic patterns do. Thus, because the divine image of God is still intact, and merely tainted or off-track, people can choose, on their own, to do acts of goodness that lead to salvation. Not only does Pelagianism mark McLaren's doctrine of creation, it influences his view of sin, too.

Though McLaren believes we need "a fresh understanding of original sin," how he defines it isn't at all fresh; it is recycled Pelagianism. Five concepts mark McLaren's view of sin, which he takes from Catholic theologian James Alison and philosophical theorist Rene Girard: Imitation, rivalry, anxiety, scapegoating, and ritualization. McLaren insists that "all human beings are caught in these subtle webs of destructive imitation, rivalry, anxiety, scapegoating, and ritualization."[29] Inherent to this definition is Pelagius' view of example and habit: "Humans beings are by nature imitative," says McLaren. "You start as my model for imitation" and "I may become the perpetrator of violence against those I envy;" "we imitate one another in violence" which produces patterns and systems of "social disintegration."[30] As I argued in chapter 3, McLaren believes sin isn't natural, but social; it is learned behavior from bad examples, which form bad habits, leading to bad systems

---

[29] McLaren, *Jesus, Moses, the Buddha, and Mohammed*, 110.

[30] McLaren, *Jesus, Moses, the Buddha, and Mohammed*, 109.

and social patterns. As McLaren says, "sin is utterly derivative, utterly imitative...there is no escape from dismal, degrading cycles of mimicry apart from a return to the creative goodness that is even more original than sin."[31] That "return to the creative (original) goodness" was provided by the better example and better pattern of living of Jesus.

Although I dealt extensively with McLaren's view of Jesus' person and work in chapter 4, it bears repeating his view of Jesus here, because of its implications in a multi-faith world. It seems clear that McLaren views Jesus as one religious figure among many, although perhaps a tad more special than the rest. In his introductory chapter, McLaren places Jesus among Moses, the Buddha, and Mohammed as "four of history's greatest religious leaders."[32] He believes that God was revealed to Jesus in the same way God was revealed to Adam, Noah, Abraham, Moses, and Mohammed, going so far as to say God spoke "to humanity through these great men and that each ones teaching and example should be trusted and followed" along with Jesus'.[33] He even thinks it ridiculous to pit Jesus as a rival against other prophets or gods or saviors, suggesting that Jesus himself would not condemn or counter other religious figures.[34] So it seems clear that for McLaren, Jesus is

---

[31] McLaren, *Jesus, Moses, the Buddha, and Mohammed*, 112.

[32] McLaren, *Jesus, Moses, the Buddha, and Mohammed*, 2.

[33] McLaren, *Jesus, Moses, the Buddha, and Mohammed*, 90.

[34] McLaren, *Jesus, Moses, the Buddha, and Mohammed*, 136.

one valid religious figure among many legitimate figures. But who is Jesus and what did he do?

In a remarkable reinterpretation of the Colossian hymn that the historic Christian faith has taken as a pivotal text teaching Jesus' deity and exclusivity, McLaren says that Jesus is "the true image of God," he is "the true embodiment of the fulness of God."[35]   As I pointed out earlier, notice that McLaren doesn't say Jesus *is* God, rather he is the *image* of God or *resembles* and is *like* God; Jesus embodies and models God in how He lives. McLaren goes on to say that Philippians —another crucial passage of Scripture the historic Christian faith has used to teach Jesus' deity—makes the point that Jesus is "a true image bearer of God," he "reveals the true nature of God." Again, McLaren isn't saying Jesus is God, merely that He *lived* like God; Jesus is the moral Son of God, not the metaphysical Son of God.

In another remarkable turn away from historic Christianity, McLaren counters the traditional meaning of the deity of Christ—"God = Jesus; Jesus = God" [36] —by cleverly reframing Christology to mean "What is true of Christ is true of God" and "God is like Christ." Rather than Jesus being God himself, He is merely a model of God, He merely images God. Thus, the incarnation is transformed from God becoming man to "Jesus embodies the divine creativity that makes impossibilities possible and that makes new possibilities spring forth into actuality." It's as if for McLaren God is merely

35 McLaren, *Jesus, Moses, the Buddha, and Mohammed*, 136-137.

36 McLaren, *Jesus, Moses, the Buddha, and Mohammed*, 139.

an idea that Jesus embodies, like Paul Tillich's (a theological liberal) view of God as the symbol of the universal human ideal. Again, rather than the actual Being of God becoming a human being, Jesus is a man who embodies "the deepest meaning" of life. As McLaren argues, "in [Jesus'] story we see the syntax of history, the plot-line of evolution, the deep meaning of the surface events, the unified field of theory that explains all data." Later, he makes this obtuse statement more clear when he says that "the true logic of the universe—the true meaning or syntax or plot-line of history—has been enfleshed in Jesus and dwelt among us..."[37] As I argued in chapter 4, for McLaren Jesus' life embodies the universal human ideal, which is love. That's what makes Him divine, not that He Himself is actually God.

So if this is who McLaren's Jesus is, what did He do? Again, I've outlined much of Jesus' works above in chapters 4 and 5, but it bears some repeating here. Because McLaren's problem hinges on the Pelagian view that the human problem is bad habits formed by bad examples and ignorance, we need a better example to form better habits in order to form better patterns and systems of living. Thus, what Jesus did was to give us a better, truer example and model to live. This work of Christ, then, is something that any person of faith can follow and accept, all the while never leaving their own religious identity.

This is why McLaren could write approvingly of his Muslim friend, who believed that Jesus was a great prophet

---

[37] McLaren, *Jesus, Moses, the Buddha, and Mohammed*, 143.

through whom God was speaking to all humanity, and that Jesus' word and example must be followed and that God would evaluate people against the measure of Jesus' life and teaching.[38] In a multi-faith world, all that matters is Jesus' loving life and example, and His words and teachings that urge humanity to pursue the universal human ideal of love.

Of course for McLaren, this call to pursue love was the crux of Jesus' greatest contribution and life work: His "community organization movement." "What did the movement do?" McLaren asks. They spread their message, looked for "people of peace" and networked them together, they fed the hungry and healed the sick, they offered hope to the depressed and promised freedom, they confronted oppressors and conversed with their critics.[39] In other words, they spread the universal human ideal of love. According to McLaren this was the saving message proclaimed by Jesus and then carried along by His followers. The saving significance of Jesus, then, was "the light of Jesus and his example." And this true light was His attitude of loving descension "into common humanity, down into servanthood, down into suffering, down into death," which in turn revealed the true nature of God.[40] As we saw in chapter 5, this loving example actually *is* our salvation, because Jesus' loving life presents an alternative system to the destructive ones of this world.

---

[38] McLaren, *Jesus, Moses, the Buddha, and Mohammed*, 135.

[39] McLaren, *Jesus, Moses, the Buddha, and Mohammed*, 233.

[40] McLaren, *Jesus, Moses, the Buddha, and Mohammed*, 137.

More specifically, what is the salvation that's inherent in McLaren's gospel, in the new kind of Christianity tailor-made for a multi-faith world? From both this book and *A New Kind of Christianity*, it seems clear McLaren's good news is the offer of the "life of Christ." And by *life of Christ* I don't meant the born-again life of the historic Christian faith, where the sinner is freed from the wages of sin, delivered from death, and literally re-created a new. I mean the model and example of Christ, the *life* of Christ.

To understand this style of salvation, it's important to understand what McLaren means by the wrath of God. Rather than God's wrath being directed toward sinners, as the Church and Scripture have taught, McLaren believes God's wrath is against "evil things." As McLaren argues, "If we speak of an angry God at all, we will speak of God angry at indifference, angry at apathy, angry at racism and violence, angry at inhumanity, angry at waste, angry at destruction, angry at injustice, angry at hostile religious clannishness."[41] McLaren makes clear God's anger is never against us, it is against "what is against us," which are the dysfunctional systems and stories of chapter 3, and things they produce.[42] In other words, "the greed, pride, fear, craving, and hostility that infect humanity" are the objects of God's wrath, not people who are greedy or prideful. And here is where salvation comes in: "and they are what God loves to save us from."

---

[41] McLaren, *Jesus, Moses, the Buddha, and Mohammed*, 259-260.

[42] McLaren, *Jesus, Moses, the Buddha, and Mohammed*, 260.

For McLaren our salvation isn't from a sinful nature, but sinful systems; we don't need salvation from death, but from life, or perhaps the bad things in life that affect us. Thus, he proclaims the salvation of his gospel is exclusive, inclusive, and universal:

> our saving message is indeed exclusive in the sense that it excludes hostility, injustice, apathy, and violence. And it is inclusive in the sense that everyone is welcome to participate, regardless of religious label. And it is universalist in the sense that it will not rest until everyone who wants to can and does experience the abundant life of shalom, humility, kindness, and justice that God desires for all.[43]

For McLaren's gospel, this last part is fundamental: He wants to share "the treasures of Christ" universally with everyone, which is Jesus' example and model of abundant life. It is in following Christ's example that we are saved, that we are liberated from the dysfunctional systems and stories of this world. Remarkably, he even claims Paul and Silas proclaimed this while in jail in Acts 16.

In this episode of Paul's missionary journeys, Paul and Silas are brought before the Roman authorities for their proselytizing activities and put in jail, where an earthquake later frees these two missionary prisoners. (It should be noted that McLaren interprets this event symbolically, arguing that the story "symbolized the earthshaking radicality of the liberating message Paul's team proclaims...") Afterwards the

---

[43] McLaren, *Jesus, Moses, the Buddha, and Mohammed*, 261.

jailer rushes in to find that his two prisoners didn't run away but stayed put. The jailer is dumbfounded and, according to McLaren, cries out "What must I do to be liberated?" Here is McLaren's interpretive paraphrase: "Paul and Silas said something like this: 'You live in the fear-based system of the Lord Caesar. Stop having confidence in him and his system of domination, hostility, and oppression. Instead, have confidence in the Lord Jesus. If you do, you and all those in your household will experience liberation."[44]

Notice McLaren doesn't say the jailer is living in rebellion to God, but living in response to the system of Caesar. Salvation, then, comes by putting confidence in Jesus' life-system, instead of Caesar's life-system. It isn't that the jailer would experience salvation from the wages of sin, which is death, but rather liberation from a bad life-system. Of course this life-system of Jesus is the Kingdom of God, which "confronts Caesar's empire of fear and death" with "liberation and reconciliation."[45] And what McLaren insists this world needs are "teams of unlikely people," Christian or not, who come together and proclaim "the way of Jesus," which is "the way of liberation;" Jesus' way, example, model of love, humility, and servanthood liberate us—save us—from the dysfunctional, destructive ways and patterns of this world. This way of Jesus is salvation, and proclaiming this way is the heart of McLaren's redefinition of Christian practices and mission.

---

[44] McLaren, *Jesus, Moses, the Buddha, and Mohammed*, 235.

[45] McLaren, *Jesus, Moses, the Buddha, and Mohammed*, 236.

The Gospel of Brian McLaren

10

RECONSTRUCTING
CHRISTIAN PRACTICES

This reformulation of doctrine has an inevitable sister act: the reconstruction of the Church's liturgical practices. Because the core doctrines of the Christian faith can no longer be conceived in ways exclusive to the Church, now the liturgy isn't even the Church's; now it's for the world. Which makes sense because the Church holds zero place in McLaren's religious enterprise. How could it? If the Church is the exclusive membership of those who've placed their faith in Jesus Christ, as the New Testament says it is, then how could such an exclusive group have any mention in such an overtly inclusive enterprise? Likewise, how could the exclusive liturgical practices of the Church remain so in such an inclusive religious reidentification exercise. They can't, beginning with Christmas Day.

Yes, you read that correctly. Now Christmas isn't even the Church's day, but humanity's day: "On Christmas Day, we would celebrate the birth of the man who repudiated the violent path of obsessive taking and blaze a new path of generous self-giving...And the celebration of Christ's birth could become a birthday party, not just for Jesus but *also for the new humanity* that transcends and includes all previous identities."[1] Now Christmas is a celebration of the new humanity, not for Jesus the Messiah.

Not only is the birth of Jesus the Messiah reformulated with a decidedly humanistic bent, other major Church holidays are, too, including Lent, Holy Week, and even Easter. For McLaren, Lent should simply be considered an annual season devoted to the life and teaching of Jesus.[2] For Palm Sunday, McLaren calls on people to join Jesus in "weeping over Jerusalem for its ignorance of the ways of peace,"[3] rather than of their ignorance and rejection of Him as their Messiah. Maundy Thursday is merely a celebration of Jesus' command to love one another.[4] Good Friday isn't the glorious day when the Son of God went to the cross as an atoning sacrifice for

---

[1] McLaren, *Jesus, Moses, the Buddha, and Mohammed*, 171.

[2] McLaren, *Jesus, Moses, the Buddha, and Mohammed*, 172.

[3] McLaren, *Jesus, Moses, the Buddha, and Mohammed*, 173.

[4] McLaren, *Jesus, Moses, the Buddha, and Mohammed*, 173.

human rebellion. Instead, it "becomes the great celebration of God's empathy with all human suffering and pain."[5]

And what of Easter? After defining miracles as something that convey "an unexpected meaning or message," McLaren goes on to say there was a scandalous meaning conveyed in the resurrection of Jesus.[6] What's important isn't that Jesus actually, physically, bodily rose from the dead. What's important is the *meaning of the story* of the risen Christ. Similarly, the meaning of the ascension is far more important than the fact of the ascension.[7] While some might be surprised by this characterization of the most important events in the church, the resurrection and the ascension, it makes sense considering McLaren's liberal roots.

For generations theological liberals have meant something very different than what the Christian faith means by the resurrection. For liberals, Jesus resurrected spiritually or existentially. Spiritually, Jesus lived on in the memory of the disciples. Existentially, Jesus lived on in the example or lives of the disciples. Similarly, for McLaren what's important isn't what happened at the tomb, but what the story of the empty tomb means, particularly for all humanity. Because according to McLaren, Easter means something "more" than "the resurrection of a single corpse—it means the ongoing resurrection of all humanity from violence to peace, from fear to faith, from hostility to love, from a culture of consumption

---

[5] McLaren, *Jesus, Moses, the Buddha, and Mohammed*, 173.

[6] McLaren, *Jesus, Moses, the Buddha, and Mohammed*, 174.

[7] McLaren, *Jesus, Moses, the Buddha, and Mohammed*, 176.

to a culture of stewardship and generosity...and in all these ways and more, from death to life."[8] So the resurrection stands as a symbol for the movement of all of humanity from that which brings death to that which brings life.

As the previous section revealed, this part carries with it an explicit universalism, in that everybody is "in" regardless of their commitment to Jesus Christ as exclusive Lord and Savior. And along with the universalism is an obvious religious pluralism, because the Christian faith and Church of Jesus Christ is not the exclusive vessel through which Christ-centered belief and practice are encountered. That universalism and pluralism is carried to its full logical conclusion in the final chapter where McLaren completely redefines Christian mission by writing the Church out of it.

---

[8] McLaren, *Jesus, Moses, the Buddha, and Mohammed*, 175.

11

REDEFINING CHRISTIAN MISSION

The heart of McLaren's redefinition of Christian mission for a multi-faith world lies in completely writing out the Church in favor of "teams of unlikely people—Christians, Jews, Muslims, Hindus, Buddhists, people from a whole range of indigenous religions, together with agnostics and atheists—coming together, not in the name of the Christian religion, but seeking to walk in the way of Jesus, learning, proclaiming, and demonstrating 'the way of liberation.'"[1] Mission for McLaren has nothing to do with the *Great Commission*, but

---

[1] McLaren, *Jesus, Moses, the Buddha, and Mohammed*, 236.

everything to do with so-called *Great Commandment* of love: Mission is spreading and sowing the universal human ideal of love—which everyone can do, whether they believe in anything at all.

The point of mission, then, is making people "a little more Christ-like," which has nothing to do with the Holy Spirit transforming people into Christ, but our shared commitment to love somehow magically influencing our behavior to reflect Jesus' loving example. After listing several people he knows who he thinks model well or fight for the universal human ideal, McLaren goes on to say "What [they] and so many other people are doing is a lot like what Jesus did: bringing together unlikely people to serve and heal together, to liberate the oppressed and their oppressors together, and to model, in their collaboration, the kind of harmony and human-kindness the world desperately needs."[2] Again, for McLaren, mission isn't about the Great Commission, but the Great Commandment.

Now, to be sure, the historic Christian faith has also been about the Great Commandment to love God and neighbor. History is riddled with examples of Christians who love the world because Christ first loved them by giving up His life, even to death on a cross. So, yes, the Christian faith is about doing acts of love, but those acts can never replace or compete with the greatest act of love we could ever give: Making disciples, baptizing them into the Church, and teaching what Jesus commanded. This is the Great Commission that Jesus

---

[2] McLaren, *Jesus, Moses, the Buddha, and Mohammed*, 247.

gave exclusively to the Church, which involves influencing people to give their life and lifestyle to Jesus as the one and only Savior and Lord; initiating people who have been saved from death to life into the Church; and teaching them how to live out the teachings of Christ through the power of the Holy Spirit. This Commission is fundamentally absent from McLaren's gospel, because the Church itself is fundamentally absent.

Stretching back to *A New Kind of Christianity* and even to *Everything Must Change*, one can see the curious absence of the Church in McLaren's religious enterprise. Instead, what's important are "religious communities...organizing for the common good."[3] Remarkably, McLaren seems to believe that any religion can solve our human problem. McLaren doesn't seem to have any issue with people of other faiths cherishing and maintaining their "distinctive religious identity." In fact, he encourages it.[4] So instead of challenging other religions to convert to faith in Jesus, we are called to band together to work toward solving our dysfunctional, destructive systems and stories by working for the common good, the commonwealth or Kingdom of God.

Because every religious identity is valid and each religion has a "unique, particular, and evolving perspective from which to encounter the Spirit in a unique way,"[5] McLaren

---

[3] McLaren, *Jesus, Moses, the Buddha, and Mohammed*, 250.

[4] McLaren, *Jesus, Moses, the Buddha, and Mohammed*, 256-257.

[5] McLaren, *Jesus, Moses, the Buddha, and Mohammed*, 152.

considers the old language of saving souls is meaningless. [6] Instead, he says our collective "sacred mission of salvation" is saving people, human societies, and this planet from "the dehumanizing effects of hostility to God and other."[7] This collective saving mission calls every individual to make a saving decision: "the choice to live not for our own selfish interests alone, and not for the groupish interests of our clan or caste or civilization alone, but for the common God, the good of all creation."[8] Since our problem is a bad way of living and our solution is the ideal way of living born by an ideal liver (Jesus), our collective human mission is to get people to live better in relationship with themselves, the Other, and the planet. And the way we do this is to issue what McLaren calls an *alter call*.

Not an *altar* call—which long-time Christians will recognize as a come-forward call to confess Jesus as Lord and Savior—but an *alter* call, a call to "consider turning around and choosing a new path," an alternate path of understanding and living. McLaren invites people to confess these things: Where they stand; who they are becoming; where they are going; how they believe; and why they believe.[9] Of course, there isn't anything particular about this confession. And frankly, it is rather humanistic, in that the confession isn't

---

[6] McLaren, *Jesus, Moses, the Buddha, and Mohammed*, 258.

[7] McLaren, *Jesus, Moses, the Buddha, and Mohammed*, 258.

[8] McLaren, *Jesus, Moses, the Buddha, and Mohammed*, 258.

[9] McLaren, *Jesus, Moses, the Buddha, and Mohammed*, 263.

rooted in God, but in the one confessing and even in humanity, in our collective power to change the world through love.

Rather than calling people to believe on the name of Jesus Christ, as the Gospels reiterate countless times, Brian seems to transform Christian missions into a humanistic call to loving action. Which makes sense because what is minimally necessary for so-called "salvation" in Brian's gospel isn't faith in Jesus, but rather faith in the universal human ideal, the idea of love, the common good. By neglecting the Church, the gospel of Jesus isn't at all unique to the Christian faith and is radically transformed from salvation from sin and death through Jesus' life, death, and resurrection. Instead, it is merely a way that liberates people from bad living, a liberation that's accessible to every person regardless of their creedal beliefs. In the end, the mission of Brian's gospel is transformed from calling people to have faith in Jesus Christ into a belief in humanity. As with every aspect of Brian's gospel, humanity is squarely at the center.

The Gospel of Brian McLaren

12

CONCLUSION

There's a fun song that's often sung in Sunday School, called "Father Abraham." Perhaps you've sung this song yourself. It goes like this:

> Father Abraham had many sons.
> Many sons had father Abraham.
> And I am one of them.
> And so are you.
> So let's all serve the Lord.
> Right arm, left arm, right foot, left foot…

The song is repeated several times, looking sillier and sillier as people move their right arm, left arm, right foot, and left foot all around. I think by the end even peoples' tongues are sticking out, which adds to the silliness as one tries to sing the words of the song! The song, of course, speaks of the reality that the Church is made of a diverse group of people who are called to serve the Lord together, as right feet and left feet, right hand and left hand, and yes even tongues. Paul reminds us that those who are in Christ, whether Jew or Gentile, are sons of Abraham who make up the Body of Christ, called to serve the world as Jesus' hands and feet.

In more theologically liberal circles, though, I've heard this song sung a different way. They sing it like so:

> Father Abraham had many sons.
> Many sons had father Abraham.
> And I am one of them.
> And so are you.
> *So let's just get along.*
> Right arm, left arm, right foot, left foot...

Did you catch the changed phrase? Rather than serving the Lord together as *one Church*, we are beckoned to "just get along" as *one humanity*. For them, every person on the planet is a son (or daughter) of father Abraham, which means we're all also sons and daughters of the *God* of Abraham—so let's just get along. This thinking reflects what J. Gresham Machen calls "the universal fatherhood of God and the universal brotherhood of man."[1] These "doctrines," as Machen called them, form the foundation to theological liberalism. They insist what McLaren insists in this newest book: that "God" is

---

[1] J. Gresham Machen, *Christianity and Liberalism* (Grand Rapids: Eerdmans Publishing, 1923), 18.

the God of everybody universally, regardless of how He is approached, worshipped, and named; that people are one in some universal religious community, regardless of their sinful condition and regardless of their beliefs or practices.

Machen makes it clear, however, that "The modern doctrine of the universal fatherhood of God is not to be found in the teaching of Jesus."[2] Furthermore, "the really distinctive New Testament teaching about the fatherhood of God concerns only those who have been brought into the household of faith."[3] In other words, while the New Testament describes God as Father, and His children relate to Him as such, those who are His children in the first place are only those who have come to the Father through Jesus Christ.[4]

Not Moses. Not the Buddha. Not Mohammed.

Jesus Christ is the only one true God through whom we are rescued and re-created. And it's unfortunate that McLaren seems to have given up on this basic, foundational belief of the Christian faith. You cannot be a "follower of God in the way of Jesus"[5] without insisting that Jesus is God Himself, and consequently that every other so-called "god" and "lord"— Buddha, Mohammed, Krishna, and all others—are not.

This was the apostle Paul's very own confession in a letter to the Church of Corinth:

---

[2] Machen, *Christianity and Liberalism*, 60.

[3] Machen, *Christianity and Liberalism*, 60.

[4] John 14:6.

[5] McLaren, *Jesus, Moses, the Buddha, and Mohammed*, 11.

> So then, about eating food sacrificed to idols: We know that "An idol is nothing at all in the world" and that "There is no God but one." For even if there are so-called gods, whether in heaven or on earth (as indeed there are many "gods" and many "lords"), yet for us there is but one God, the Father, from whom all things came and for whom we live; and there is but one Lord, Jesus Christ, through whom all things came and through whom we live.[6]

Paul makes it clear that at least for Christians, there is one God, the Father; one Lord, Jesus Christ. Here Paul is quoting a portion of the cornerstone to the Jewish faith, the *Shema*—Hear, O Israel, the Lord, the Lord is one[7]—and redefining it to refer to Jesus Christ. In other words, the one God who created all things is Jesus Christ. Those "so-called gods" and "so-called lords" are neither of the two. They are fake. Jesus and Jesus alone is the only real God and Lord.

This would have been as radical in Paul's day as it is in ours to suggest there is no God or Lord but Jesus Christ. In Paul's day you couldn't travel anywhere in the Roman empire without being confronted by the multi-faith and multi-god nature of the world. Every city had its own god. Every part of creation itself—from the seas to war to agriculture—had its own god. Yet, at every turn in Paul's ministry he insists that Jesus and Jesus alone is the only one true God.

---

[6] 1 Corinthians 8:4-6.

[7] Deuteronomy 6:4.

So why wouldn't we do the same in our day? Is ours really all that different than Paul's?

One day while Paul was on one of his missionary journeys, he stopped in Athens to wait for Silas and Timothy to join him. As he impatiently wandered the streets "he was greatly distressed to see that the city was full of idols." A Roman nobleman, Pliny the Elder, estimated the Greek city of Rhodes had 73,000 statues of multiple gods and insisted that Athens had no fewer. So it's understandable why Paul was so distraught and distressed!

And how did he respond? Did he claim that "something good still shines from the heart" of those religious shrines and artifacts, as McLaren would insist?[8] While Paul did commend the Athenians for their religiosity, he also called them "ignorant"—twice![9] And he insisted that, while God in the past had overlooked such ignorant religious living and worship, now He was calling people to repent from their idolatry, "For he has set a day when he will judge the world with justice by the man he has appointed. He has given proof of this to everyone by raising him from the dead."[10] Of course "the man" is Jesus. It is by Jesus that people from every false religion on the planet will be judged, whether in Him or not in Him. And Paul called on them to believe in Jesus.

I wish that McLaren would make the same call to his friends from other religions. For we know from Scripture that

---

[8] McLaren, *Jesus, Moses, the Buddha, and Mohammed*, 20.

[9] Acts 17:23, 30.

[10] Acts 17:31.

rescue from sin and death is found in no one else but Jesus Christ—"there is no other name under heaven given to mankind by which we must be saved."[11]

Not Moses'. Not the Buddha's. And not Mohammed's.

---

[11] Acts 4:12.

AFTERWORD

If I have learned anything over the years in my academic pursuits it's this: theology matters. Getting the "pieces" of theology right, as much as we can in our finiteness, matters because when we get one of those pieces "wrong," the rest fall in lockstep.

How one defines our human problem has great bearing on how one defines our human solution. How one defines our human solution has great bearing on how one defines the One who bore that solution. This book has demonstrated as much in its overview of the generational development of Protestant liberal theology. When you define our human problem environmentally, then our solution must do something with our environment; when you define our human problem as having to do with bad examples, then our solution must provide a better example; when you define our human problem as narratively driven, then our solution must provide a better narrative to live and lean into.

Perhaps more significantly, our definition of the One who bore our solution, Jesus of Nazareth, is reduced to a prophet-like character who came simply to provide us a better example and better story to live; He came to change our environment in order to change us. So what's important about Jesus becomes His life and way of living. This means He doesn't have to be God and doesn't have to actually be alive.

If I have learned anything in the last few years, it's that theology matters, and when you get the pieces of theology wrong you ultimately get the gospel wrong. Of late, my generation is all a flutter with reimagining the Christian faith —reimagining the pieces of the Christian faith. I understand this pull toward reimagining the Christian faith, because I have been there myself. But what I have learned as I have journeyed into, through, and beyond the Emergent Church and gospel of Brian McLaren is that what my generation needs is not to reimagine the Christian faith, but rediscover it. We need to rediscover what and how the Church of Jesus Christ has always believed about our problem, solution, and the One who bore that solution. We need to rediscover the gospel.

To be frank, that rediscovery effort is not going to come through the Emergent Church generally and Brian McLaren specifically. It is clear their reimagination enterprise is simply one iteration in a long line of Protestant liberal leavers— Emergents have left the historic Christian faith in the same way liberals have every generation since Schleiermacher, yet in a way that's palatable for our postmodern, post-Christian day. Which, for this post-Emergent who had high hopes of a genuine third way that cuts through the malaise of contemporary liberal-conservative theologic discourse, is sad indeed.

This book on McLaren's gospel is deeply personal. It's personal because I myself was involved with and hoodwinked by the Emergent Church. And it's personal because I myself still long for a third way. I realize this term is over used, yet as I survey our current evangelical landscape that is split between progressive Emergent evangelicals on the one side and traditional Young Calvinist evangelicals on the other, I'm left wanting. I—and my gut tells me plenty more people—want an alternative that cuts through the current evangelical malaise and recaptures the gospel in all of its grandeur and majesty and revolutionary character—a gospel that includes the Kingdom in all of its already-not-yet glory in order to provide new life right now and is still exclusively tied to the only one true God, Jesus Christ.

Now more than ever the Church is in need of passionate ambassadors of Christ who take seriously their calling as ministers of reconciliation, in the fullest sense of that Kingdom calling. Yet, I hope that a new generation of Christians will rediscover what the Church has always believed regarding God's magical, revolutionary Story of Rescue in order to bring the type of right-now transformation for which our world longs—without reimagining the Kingdom for, and consequently the gospel, along the way.

What the Church—and even the world—does not need now is a new kind of Christianity for our multi-faith world. What the Church needs is the old, old gospel Story of Jesus and His radical, furious love.

FIVE GENERATIONS OF LIBERAL *KINGDOM* GRAMMAR

"In this important guide, Jeremy Bouma explains how many who speak of the Kingdom of God do not mean what Jesus meant by it. If you are one who is attracted to the liberal gospel, this guide might just save your soul." —MICHAEL E. WITTMER, Grand Rapids Theological Seminary

In recent years the use of Kingdom of God language has markedly increased within evangelicalism, and rightly so, as the Kingdom is central to the teachings of Jesus. While recapturing this aspect of the Christian faith is a good thing, several scholars have noted similarities between such language and Protestant liberalism. These

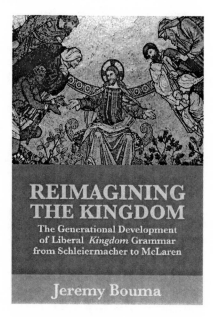

REIMAGINING THE KINGDOM

The Generational Development of Liberal *Kingdom* Grammar from Schleiermacher to McLaren

Jeremy Bouma

scholars, however, have not significantly explored these similarities or the impact liberal Kingdom grammar is having on evangelical notions of the Kingdom.

REIMAGINING THE KINGDOM traces the development of Kingdom grammar through four generations of liberalism —from Schleiermacher to Ritschl, Rauschenbusch, and Tillich —in order to understand how such grammar is affecting evangelical theology, particularly the variety espoused by so-called "Emergent" progressive evangelicals. By exploring how theological liberals define the human problem, understand that problem's solution, and interpret the nature of the One who bore that solution, this book reveals an inextricable link between progressive Emergent evangelicalism and Protestant liberalism.

As with liberal Kingdom grammar, progressive evangelicals ultimately urge people to place their faith in the way of Jesus—i.e. the Kingdom of God— rather than the person and work of Jesus. This is a significant departure from authentic, historic Christianity. Therefore, it is imperative that evangelicals understand the contours of liberal Kingdom grammar in order to understand how such grammar is affecting how some evangelicals understand, show, and tell the gospel itself.

CPSIA information can be obtained at www.ICGtesting.com
Printed in the USA
LVOW11s1504010816

498603LV00004B/384/P